MENTAL HEALTH AND AUTHORITARIANISM ON THE COLLEGE CAMPUS

Gerald Amada

University Press of America™

Copyright © 1979 by

University Press of America, Inc.™

4710 Auth Place, S.E., Washington, D.C. 20023

ISBN: 0-8191-0831-6
Library of Congress Number: 79-66480

To the memory of my mother, Rose Amada

and to my father, Samuel Amada

who taught me the importance of love and perseverance

ACKNOWLEDGMENTS

This book is a natural outgrowth of the efforts of a great many organizations and individuals who have provided invaluable assistance to the City College of San Francisco Mental Health Program since 1970. The Zellerbach Family Fund and its Executive Director, Ed Nathan, provided generous financial and moral support in order to first establish the program in 1970.

The Westside Mental Health Center of San Francisco, under the outstanding leadership of Dr. William Goldman, provided supplemental funding and enthusiastic assistance to the program in its earliest years.

The Bothin Helping Fund of San Francisco and its Vice-President, Ms. Genevieve di San Faustino, provided subvention and enthusiastic encouragement to the Mental Health Program at a time when it was faced with serious cutbacks and possible dissolution.

Progress Foundation, Inc. of San Francisco and its chief administrators, Dr. Patricia Caughey, Steve Harover and Steve Fields, gave unstintingly of their time and energy in behalf of the Mental Health Program in its formative years.

To all of these organizations and individuals I wish to express my heartfelt thanks and gratitude.

I also owe a great debt of gratitude to the staff,

faculty and students of City College for the precious confidence and trust they have placed in their mental health service.

The Board of Governors of City College deserves special acknowledgment and may take pride in the enlightened and progressive leadership it has provided to the Mental Health Program since the inception of the program.

I am extremely appreciative of the editorial efforts of Dr. Myra Wise, Dr. Aiko Oda, and Dr. George Fuller, each of whom painstakingly and sympathetically reviewed and evaluated the manuscript for this book. The book's flaws and deficiencies are my own doing and responsibility, but many of its strong points must be credited to the help provided by these three generous individuals.

Two persons deserve special thanks and acknowledgment. Alan Leavitt provided this study with indispensable information and insight. For this assistance and for all-important career opportunities he extended to me over ten years ago, I am deeply indebted to this far-sighted and creative man.

This book could not have been written without Myrna Quan Holden, Co-Director of the Mental Health Program. Myrna deserves special recognition and appreci-

ation, not only for providing me with essential aid with
this study, but for the many years she has bolstered me
with her unique sensitivity, intelligence and courage.
I consider myself uniquely privileged to be her close
colleague and friend.

I am indebted to Amelia Lippi, secretary of the
Mental Health Program, not only for her remarkable contribution to the program, but for the great care and kind-
ness with which she has always treated me.

I am of course profoundly grateful to my family,
Marcia, Robin, Naomi, Laurie and Eric for the love, joy
and humor with which they have sustained me. The setbacks and tribulations which are described in this book
were always made easier by knowing that I would end each
day among my loving family.

                              Gerald Amada
                              San Francisco, CA   1979

FOREWORD

The reader will perhaps find this book more understandable and cogent if first offered a few explanatory caveats. First, throughout the book I will strongly emphasize those institutional events in the development of a college mental health program which were largely characterized by conflict, between individuals as well as between organizational factions.

Such a characterization might cause the reader to validly raise the following questions. "Why not, for the sake of balance and perspective, discuss those institutional events which were relatively positive and free of conflict? Is it not tendentious to examine so minutely and exclusively instances of strife and discord, rather than instances of harmony, cooperation and consonance?"

My rejoinder to these valid questions is two-pronged. First, the two principal organizational factions which are discussed in this study - the mental health service and the highest levels of the college administration - rarely enjoyed prolonged "harmony" or "cooperation" with each other. This fact, as the reader will note in the text, was repeatedly and publicly acknowledged by both sides, paradoxically producing one of the few points upon which each could unreservedly agree. Therefore, to place emphasis upon the role and significance of cooperation and accord between the mental health program and the college administration would be to inexcusably sugarcoat the facts and produce a study which perforce would suffer from historical inexactitude.

Second, I believe that, in order to learn about and achieve states of harmony and "normalcy," one must first study that which is pathological (in individuals) or, to use a term coined by one of the authors quoted in this book, bureaupathic (in social organizations). In other words, I think we have more to learn from difficult and disharmonious experiences than from our relishable successes. This stance is one which Anna Freud once aptly described as the "profitable nature of negative experience."

One further note of explanation. Besides myself, only two persons in this book are identified by name; all others by titular designation. Aside from the two persons identified by name, (who, incidentally, readily gave their permission to be so identified) there was no conscientious attempt on my part to either completely conceal or divulge the actual identities of those other persons mentioned in this study. I did not seek permission for use of their names from the many unnamed persons who are included in this book for the following reasons: (1) Such an undertaking would be inordinately time-consuming, (2) Because of the nature of the study and its characterizations, permission for name usage would undoubtedly be denied by many of the principals, and (3) Identification by name for such a large cast of characters would, in my estimation, do little to enhance the readability or credibility of the study.

The reader may, after reading this book, be interested to learn that the Dean of Students and the Chancellor-Superintendent referred to in the text no longer occupy those positions. The former has received a promotion in the same college and the latter has retired.

Due to the emotionally painful memories it sometimes revived, the writing of this book was often a torrid personal experience, suffused with a good deal of anguish and rage. Nevertheless, I can easily admit that this undertaking has fundamentally been a labor of love which I hope will serve to further improve the academic institution to which I am deeply devoted and indebted.

Gerald Amada

INTRODUCTION

This is a case study of an educational institution with the establishment of the mental health program as a critical event in the history of that institution. The primary focus of this study will be upon the following:

(1) the interaction between the Mental Health Program and other departments and services of the college;

(2) the interaction between the Mental Health Program and the college administration;

(3) the interaction between the Mental Health Program and community mental health agencies;

(4) the nature of intraagency relationships within the Mental Health Program;

(5) the role of City College students as both consumers and advisors of the Mental Health Program.

The data for this study will be gathered from the following sources:

(1) relevant publications which deal with college mental health services, the epidemiology of the mental health problems of college students, the character of modern organizations, and the various styles of administrative leader-

ship;

(2) personal interviews with some of the principals who were involved in the development
of the Mental Health Program;

(3) memoranda, correspondence, and summary reports which illuminate historical develop-
ments in the Mental Health Program;

(4) local newspaper articles about the Mental
Health Program; and

(5) my own personal recollection of the events
which transpired.

The data included in this study will be analyzed
from the following theoretical frameworks:

(1) the psychoanalytic model which enhances our
understanding of the authoritarian personality from the standpoint of his defense mechanisms and personality charecteristics;

(2) the organizational model which studies modern
organizations as entities which, over time,
naturally ossify and ritualistically tend
toward "bureaupathic" resistances to change.

Although this study will not be conducted without
a degree of personal impression and bias, there will be
every effort to present the facts accurately and fairly.
A shortcoming to the narrational approach of this study

xiv

will be a tendency to overhighlight certain events and viewpoints and a converse tendency to underplay certain other relevant events and perspectives. Nevertheless, there is a plethora of valid resources and material from which to derive factual data about the Mental Health Program and, therefore, I have every expectation that this study will be a thorough and comprehensive one. Since the study is basically a retrospective one, I have the luxury of establishing certain points of view with the benefit of hindsight. Yet it would not be untrue to mention that many of the opinions posited in this study were held, consciously or unconsciously, in my mind in 1970, the year of the inception of the Mental Health Program.

I wish to readily acknowledge that this study will be pervaded with the social values to which I adhere, both in my private and professional life. Since value-free social research has long been questioned as an attainable or even desirable objective, I believe my own set of social values will serve to enhance the quality of this study.

TABLE OF CONTENTS

xvii

THE ORIGINS OF THE MENTAL HEALTH PROGRAM

Statement of Purpose

I will attempt to describe and explain the
complex process of establishing and maintaining a
mental health service on an urban community college
campus -- City College of San Francisco. Although
the strategies, interventions and techniques which
sustained and fortified the Mental Health Program
throughout its history were largely adopted in an
ad hoc manner, this study will attempt to offer a
theoretical perspective of how institutions and human
personalities behave and interact with each other.

City College of San Francisco

City College of San Francisco is a two-year
community college of approximately 16,000 day students
and 9,500 evening students. It has an open admissions
policy and no fees. It offers two basic programs:
(1) an academic curriculum designed to enable students

to transfer to a four-year college or university; and
(2) vocational and semiprofessional training programs,
including police science, dental assistance, and hotel/
restaurant management. Particular emphasis in recent
years has been placed upon the recruitment and tutoring
of disadvantaged people who would otherwise not attend
college.

City College, like other urban community
colleges, has a student population which reflects the
diversity of the city itself. Statistics for the Fall
of 1976 semester indicate that more than one-half of
the students were from ethnic minorities. Twenty-two
per cent were Asian, 14 per cent Black, 15 per cent
Latino and La Raza, and 2 per cent were Native American, Samoan, or other than Caucasian. Over 20 per cent
of all City College students receive some form of public
assistance. In 1970 (the year of the inception of the
Mental Health Program) 17 per cent of all students had
family incomes under $300 per month; another 15 per
cent had total family incomes ranging from $301 to $500
per month.

Presently, the average age of students at City
College is 25. As Carey and Rogers (1973) point out,
this youthful, urban student population is a group
which is particularly susceptible to a variety of medi-

2

cal and social problems, including venereal disease, drug and alcohol abuse, and unwanted pregnancy. Many City College students have grown up in racial ghettos or poverty areas, and large numbers are handicapped by linguistic and cultural backgrounds that are sharply different from the White, middle class world they are entering, usually for the first time, as college students. These differences are often compounded by financial and personal problems, poor housing, criminal records, heavy drug use, an impulsive live-for-the-moment orientation developed in reaction to the largely ungratifying world in which they have always lived, and many years of experiencing schools as hostile and frustrating places.

For the younger student, City College represents a transition from high school to the assumption of an adult role in the community. In addition to mounting responsibilities, the student will have to cope with the complexities of sexual liberation and the prevalent use of drugs -- issues around which he must develop a personal philosophy and courage. The older student may face a different set of dilemmas: academic skills may be rusty, although a wealth of personal experience can be a great asset. Yet all students will face a formidable world, often with much uncertainty and fear.

3

Currently, there are approximately 2,300
students who have graduated from foreign high schools,
many of them quite recently. This group in particular
is susceptible to cultural identity crises characterized by social isolation and severe anxiety as a result of contradictory cultural roles and expectations.

The City of San Francisco

City College is strongly shaped and affected by
the city in which it is located. San Francisco, like
so many other large American cities, is constantly
undergoing many processes of social change. Due to
its geography and its status as a West Coast port, San
Francisco has some unique social problems. The city's
1975 population of 776,000 is crowded into 45.4 square
miles: the highest population density in the state and
one of the highest in the nation (14,707 per square
mile).

San Francisco is unique in its multi-racial and
ethnic mix with more "other nonwhite" than Black population. Ethnic group estimates for 1975 follow the
trends experienced during the decade 1960 to 1970, with
a decrease, 61,186 or 12.0% in the White population and
an increase of 13,212 or 6.5% in the nonwhite groups
in 1975 over 1970. Blacks gained nearly 1 1/2 per cent,

4

while the Chinese showed a numerical increase of 4,504, Filipinos 4,406 and the other nonwhite group 1,985.

Although San Francisco has a declining population (47,974 or 6.7% from April 1, 1970), it suffers from chronic housing and job shortages. In addition to changes in the ethnic composition of the city's population, there have been other changes in the city's population structure. San Francisco's residents are becoming, synchronously, younger and older. San Francisco consistently has a higher death rate than California and surrounding counties chiefly because of the age structure of its population. In 1975, almost 15% of its population was at least 65 years of age.

Also reflecting the age and ethnic composition of the city are the leading causes of death for its residents. While the four leading causes of death (diseases of the heart, malignant neoplasms, cerebrovascular disease and accidents) are the same as those statewide and nationally, it is significant that the fifth leading cause of death in the city is cirrhosis of the liver. This compares with a seventh rank nationally and a sixth rank in California for this disease. Suicide is the seventh leading cause of death in San Francisco, as compared to its tenth rank nationally.

5

In 1975, San Francisco had one of the highest case rates of tuberculosis in the country. Statistics of the Department of Public Health reveal an overall case rate of 51.7 per 100,000 (345 cases), with the Filipino (226.8 per 100,000) and Chinese (101.3 per 100,000) ethnic groups showing the highest rates of this disease.

In the late 1960's, San Francisco was a leading center of counter-culture activity. Thousands of young people descended upon the city in hopes of a better life than was offered in the suburbs of America. Unfortunately, many personal tragedies resulted from the huge influx of teenage youth. Harassment from the law enforcement agencies left many with criminal records. Others suffered from severe drug abuse and the terror instilled by the oppressively open sexual mores which prevailed in the groups with which they associated. Many are still struggling to re-enter the mainstream of the economic and social systems. Some of that once rebellious group are now students of City College.

Theoretical Framework

As indicated earlier, I will attempt to delineate and interpret the manifold forces which influenced the outcome of the Mental Health Program (which I shall

6

henceforth refer to as MHP) from a particular theoretical perspective. I will posit a theoretical framework which will provide a perspective of formal contemporary organizations as social and political entities which are intrinsically and ineluctably torn between the contending forces of humanism and authoritarianism.

Victor Thompson (1971) comments on the humanistic underpinnings of formal organizations when he states,

> Modern bureaucratic organization is the most productive arrangement of human effort that man has thus far contrived. Its ability to accomplish objective organizational goals has produced the highest standard of living yet achieved by man. (p. 466)

He also concedes that certain "bureaupathic" (authoritarian) tendencies emerge in bureaucratic organizations, as they become specialized, such as excessive aloofness, ritualistic attachment to routines and procedures, and resistance to change; and associated with these behavior patterns is a petty insistence upon the rights of authority and status. These behavior patterns, which surface with marked regularity in formal organizations, have been described as some of the recognizable characteristics of authoritarianism by Adorno, *et al.* (1966).

Tannenbaum (1966) acknowledges that a bureaucratic organization humanistically defines the rules of the game

so as to restrict the prerogatives of the
superior within legitimate, job-essential bounds,
guaranteeing equal treatment for all subordinates. Rational and objective criteria, such as
seniority or tested competence -- not personal
preference by the superior -- are, *theoretically*,
the bases for advancement.
(Emphasis added; pp 8-9)

Tannenbaum also affirms the authoritarianism of

bureaucratic organizations when he asserts that the for-

mal organization is

set up to minimize -- if not to eliminate --
disruptions caused by personality and individual
idiosyncracy. It does not make a bit of difference from the point of view of formal organization
who performs a given role, provided his behaviors
are appropriate and conforming. (p. 5)

Quintessentially formal organizations are com-

posed of replaceable members and, clearly, impersonal

replaceability is an unmistakable hallmark of authori-

tarianism.

Bennis (1969) states that the bureaucratic mecha-

nism, so capable of coordinating men and power in a sta-

ble society of routine tasks, cannot cope with the human-

istic ethos of twentieth century conditions. Thus, the

typical contemporary bureaucratic solution to the problem

of integrating individual needs and management goals is

to regard the individual as a passive instrument (author-

itarianism), rather than as a complex being with rising

expectations (humanism). The bureaucratic solution to

the problem of the distribution of power is the implicit

8

use of coercive authority rather than education and a shared decision-making process. The bureaucratic solution to the problem of resolving conflicts is the exploitation of "loyalty" rather than reliance on competence and professionalism. Pffifner and Sherwood (1960) state the case more succinctly when they refer to the large-scale organization as potentially "a standardizing enemy of human dignity."

Erving Goffman (1961) draws attention to the struggle between humanistic and authoritarian values in "total institutions" such as the mental hospital. Although the psychiatric hospital is explicitly founded and operated to provide humanistically for the care, safety and psychological well-being of troubled inmates, they frequently place their unfortunate charges in a position of "self-alienating moral servitude." In supporting the authoritarian occupational role of those who administer the hospitals, psychiatric patients are "crushed by the weight of a service ideal that eases life for the rest of us."

I express skepticism over the exuberant assumption that child-care agencies, institutions which are officially dedicated to protecting and nurturing children, are actually fulfilling their humanistic goals.

> There is a fallacious and dangerous common assumption that child-care agencies which are legally licensed, well financed and which enjoy longevity and "respectability," are decent places for children. (Amada, 1972, p. 37)

The following were some of the organizational problems of the child-care agency which were identified: (1) a tendency of administrators to carry out decisions in a coercive manner, (2) an uncooperative attitude on the part of administrators toward the recommendations of referring agencies for therapeutic planning and rehabilitation, and (3) institutional racism as manifested in a policy of refusing admission of minority children to the child-care program.

In referring to the plight of administrators of colleges and universities, organizations which are universally committed to humanistic ideals, William Moore (1971), a former community college president, suggests that higher education has two (anti-humanistic) goals for administrators: overwork them; turn them into vassals.

Theoretical Frame of Reference

In the present study, I will describe, analyze and interpret the historical organization of the MHP from a sociopolitical perspective which stresses the recurrent and intense confrontations between the authoritarian and humanistic trends which are inherent in

10

formal organizations. I believe that this frame of reference will enable the reader to appreciate the enormous complexities which must be dealt with in establishing a mental health program on a college campus.

Origins of the Mental Health Program

The MHP had its obscure genesis in the Student Health Service (SHS) of City College. In 1968, the SHS was staffed by only one health practitioner, a public health nurse (PHN). Although her official responsibilities were to provide medical-nursing services exclusively, the PHN was continually besieged by students who were plagued with a wide variety of complex psychological difficulties. Her plaint, at that time, was that the only available means of assisting those students was by means of referring them to community psychiatric clinics, a procedure which was frequently undesirable and abortive. In her own words, referring students in psychological crisis to off-campus agencies too often meant:

> time-consuming searches for proper assistance, long waiting lists, endless red-tape and financial hassles. In addition, many students have found the process of applying for services elsewhere an awesomely formidable challenge, due to feelings of self-stigma, which they would prefer to avoid. Usually, by the time adequate assistance has materialized, it has been too late, and

11

> the student's whole semester is at stake; one
> factor which accounts for the unusually high
> rates of leaves of absence each semester.

Based upon the PHN's own findings, which were solidly substantiated by available epidemiological research of college students on other campuses, a demonstration project was conducted in the Spring of 1969. The objectives of the demonstration project were: (1) to centralize psychological services on campus, and (2) to determine the extent of potential utilization of such a program. To implement this study, a third-year psychiatric resident with the San Francisco Mental Health Services was assigned to the SHS for the Spring 1969 semester. His responsibilities included (a) direct psychological services to students, (b) consultation services to the PHN, faculty and administration in dealing with the emotional problems of students, and (c) psychiatric liaison services to community agencies to facilitate mutual referrals of students for psychotherapy.

The SHS maintained an open intake policy, seeing all students who applied and seeing them soon after application. The psychiatric resident spent the majority of his time in direct psychotherapeutic work with students. He also spent a generous amount of time in consultation with college personnel. Deliberately, minimal time was allotted to activities such as admission pro-

12

cessing, history-taking, psychological assessment and record keeping (1969).

At the end of the Spring semester, 98 different students had been served by the program. This group received a total of 253 sessions. Although these 98 students comprised only a miniscule proportion of the total number of 14,000 day students enrolled in 1969, these figures are impressive for several reasons: (1) the program was new and its whereabouts relatively unknown; (2) the psychiatric resident, who was the sole provider of psychological services, was new to the campus himself and had little time to familiarize himself with those programs and personnel which could serve as effective sources of student referrals to the SHS (as was often pointed out in subsequent years, vast numbers of college personnel knew virtually nothing of the pilot study which was conducted in 1969); and (3) as Farnsworth (1964) suggests, the extent to which students utilize the SHS will depend in part on the manner in which they perceive the service and its usefulness to them. Since one semester was clearly too abbreviated a period of time in which to engender student trust in the credibility and usefulness of the program, the intake figures for the Spring semester of 1969 were not regarded as a valid index of future utilization of the psychological services.

Based upon the relative success of the demonstration project, the PHN next proceeded to contact major community hospitals and psychiatric clinics, hoping to enlist their support in organizing and staffing a formal mental health clinic on campus. The earliest responses from personnel of these organizations were friendly to the concept of an on-campus psychological service at City College, but quite unreceptive to bearing certain practical sacrifices in order to bring such a program to fruition. At best, those agencies intimated that they could provide consultation services to college personnel, if such a bilateral arrangement were practicable.

In March of 1969, the PHN received an encouraging letter from the Chief Psychiatric Social Worker of Mt. Zion Hospital, San Francisco, in which she was advised that the request for community assistance was being referred to the California Medical Clinic for Psychotherapy (CMCP), a private non-profit psychiatric clinic (1969). Both Mt. Zion Hospital and CMCP were members of a consortium of agencies: the Westside Community Mental Health Services (WCMHS), which was founded in 1968. The request was referred to CMCP because it had already been in the business of providing consultation services to schools which were located in the WCMHS "catchment" area. The administrative director of CMCP had already made several preliminary overtures, in 1968, to the City College administration, with the intent of establishing an on-campus mental health service. Regrettably, a tentative proposal which was submitted in 1968 to establish such a program was rescinded due to jurisdictional entanglements (the college was geographically outside the WCMHS district).

After several joint meetings in May, 1969 between the psychiatric resident, the PHN, the administrative director of CMCP and members of the college administration, a plan was formulated to submit a grant proposal to the Zellerbach Family Fund in San Francisco. The requisite and much encouraged inclusion of college administrative staff in these early meetings exemplified the sound administrative principle that "no mental health program should be started by a college until or unless it has the solid backing of the administration" (Farnsworth, 1957).

In October, 1969 the Zellerbach Family Fund awarded a grant in the amount of $24,000 to be used over an 18 month period to establish and operate a "demonstration" on-campus mental health service. Subsequently, the original grant was supplemented by an additional grant of $41,000 from the National Institute of Mental Health (NIMH). The NIMH monies were funneled

15

through the administrative aegis of the WCMHS which,
together with CMCP, assumed joint responsibility for
the allocation of all funds and co-sponsorship of the
MHP. The MHP began serving students on the first day
of school in January, 1970.

The administrative and clinical staff of the MHP
functioned within the constellation of a multilateral
and, at times, highly ambiguous, system of accountability. Three rather disparate organizations simultaneously
assumed a degree of official authority over the MHP in
1970. (See organization chart, on page 18)

The Westside Community Mental Health Services

The WCMHS was initially a consortium of nine private, voluntary agencies which was established in 1968
to provide a full range of mental health services to
every resident of the district. The population of the
district numbers about 180,000 people, and includes the
quite affluent neighborhoods of Pacific Heights, the
most alienated ghettos of the Fillmore, Haight-Ashbury,
Japan Town; and many blocks of middle class neighborhoods (1968). The range of mental health programs in
the WCMHS district included psychiatric outpatient services, in-patient care, day hospital treatment and emer-
gency care 24 hours a day. Although eligibility for

16

these programs was extended to all district residents, the low-cost services provided by many of the member agencies were manifestly most useful to those persons who were socially and economically disadvantaged, especially members of minority groups.

The WCMHS was governed by a board of directors to which an Executive Director was administratively accountable. The Executive Director delegated administrative authority to a number of assistant directors, including the Assistant Director for Clinical Services. The Assistant Director for Clinical Services, in turn, bore immediate administrative responsibility for overseeing the City College MHP. Thus, the Administrative Director of the MHP was directly answerable to the WCMHS Assistant Director for Clinical Services. The fact that WCMHS was committed primarily to the mental health needs of the disadvantaged and ethnic minorities of the Westside district mandated a special set of demands and expectations of the City College MHP which will be examined in detail later in this report.

The California Medical Clinic for Psychotherapy

The California Medical Clinic for Psychotherapy (CMCP) was founded in 1959, primarily to provide long-term psychotherapy to middle income residents throughout

CITY COLLEGE OF SAN FRANCISCO - MENTAL HEALTH PROGRAM
ORGANIZATION CHART - 1970

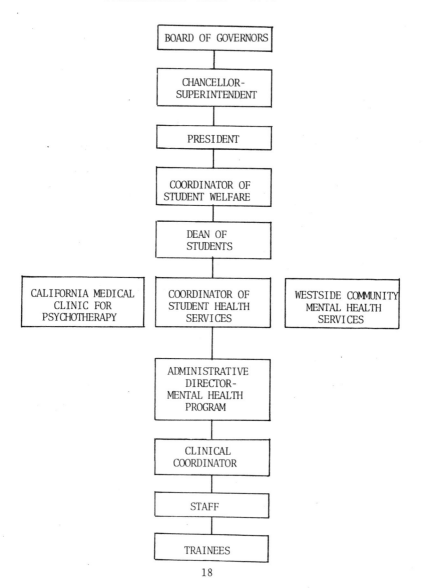

the Bay Area. The CMCP historically gave clinical priority to a clientele which could neither economically qualify for governmentally subsidized psychological services nor financially afford high cost private psychotherapy, i.e., the middle income client. This clientele was preponderantly employed and employable and Caucasian.

In 1970, the CMCP was directed by a governing board of directors, to which a Medical Director and Administrative Director, serving as administrative co-equals, were accountable. Not coincidentally, as indicated earlier, the Administrative Director of CMCP, in a two-hatted fashion, served concurrently as the first Administrative Director of the City College MHP. Within the context of this somewhat idiosyncratic arrangement it would not be an exaggeration to say that he was directly accountable only to himself. The truth of this impression will be corroborated by his comments which will be included in this report.

The San Francisco Community College District

A third organization which imposed a hierarchical system of accountability upon the MHP was, naturally, the Community College District of the City of San Francisco. The Community College District, which includes both the

19

decentralized "satellite" centers of instruction and the
centralized academic programs of the City College campus,
is governed by a Board of Governors which is elected by
the citizens of San Francisco. The administrator of
both the City College campus and the Community Centers
is the Chancellor-Superintendent. The highest administrative official of the City College campus is the President, who is immediately responsible to the Chancellor-
Superintendent. The Administrative Director of the MHP
was, at least within the organizational structure of
City College, accountable to the PHN. The Dean of Students was the primary administrative link between the
PHN and the President.

The highest priority of City College has been to
make readily available to maximum populations of the
City of San Francisco the opportunity to attain a satisfactory college education. Particular emphasis has been
given to energetically and innovatively reaching and
helping the educationally and economically disadvantaged,
especially those from minority groups. In that respect,
City College and WCMHS might appear to have kindred and
compatible organizational spirits and objectives. Yet
the provision of formal on-campus mental health services
for City College students, particularly before 1970,
had been considered a low priority issue by the highest

officials of the college administration. Basically, the perceptions of the then Chancellor-Superintendent and President had been that educational pursuits and psychological well being were two rather unrelated and unmeshable matters.

The Administrative Director of the Mental Health Program

The diversity of social philosophies and programmatic priorities among the three organizations which governed and dynamically impinged upon the MHP produced an administrative quagmire which required special navigational skills on the part of the Administrative Director of the MHP, Mr. Alan Leavitt. Although each sponsoring agency was committed to a particular, albeit different, set of humanistic goals, Mr. Leavitt, as the most central figure in this organizational configuration, had to determine how he would fulfill his mandate to establish a well integrated and relatively autonomous program which was a totally unique component within each of the parent organizations. Since he had to deal with many contradictory organizational values and priorities, it would have been pointless and self-defeating to try to steadfastly satisfy the incompatible requirements of those respective organizations. For that matter, as Etzioni (1964, p. 25) submits, "Only the naive, inexperienced administrator would assume that orders properly issued will as a rule be properly carried out." Since he was neither naive nor inexperienced, how did Mr. Leavitt resolve this dilemma?

In short, he astutely treated administrative ambiguities and overlappings as an impetus and asset to his freedom to act independently. Rather than regard the prerogatives of the governing agencies as sacred cows, he creatively maintained considerable administrative latitude by relying upon their confidence in his judgment or their diffidence in challenging his decisions. For example, none of the sponsoring organizations ventured to impose conditions or restrictions upon the process of hiring mental health program staff. Consequently, Mr. Leavitt single-handedly took responsibility for recruiting and orienting all of the original clinical staff of the MHP. He also exercised almost complete control over the development of program policies and priorities.

In his own words, the nebulous administrative structure allowed him, in many important respects, to "do as I damned pleased." In describing his relationship to the CMCP, he asserts that he was in an extremely advantageous position to act in an unhindered manner.

I came to CMCP in 1965, at a time when it was in

financial straits and, as a one-man show, I reorganized the clinic into a highly successful organization. On the basis of that achievement there was general respect at the CMCP for my competence. The Board and staff of CMCP saw the college MHP as my toy. They figured that I liked it, I was having fun with it, it was a good community thing and it didn't cost them any money since the MHP grant reimbursed them for my salary. They were not in a position to question whatever I wanted to do so long as it didn't cost them any money and so long as the clinic ran well and I managed to work it out in such a way to see that that happened.

In discussing the CMCP's apparent acquiescence to his authority during this period, Mr. Leavitt admits, without reservation, that there were several areas of subtle organizational resistance to the MHP.

As a powerful member of the Board, the Medical Director, rather indirectly and guardedly, raised two questions about the MHP (which were later to have major repercussions for the MHP).

One of his qualms was that the MHP would divert the clinical energies of Mr. Leavitt, to the detriment of CMCP. The second reservation he held, which ultimately proved to be a more lethal factor to the MHP, was that he himself had not been recruited to professionally serve in this new and attractive program.

In order to assuage any fears that he would neglect the CMCP, Mr. Leavitt gave repeated assurances, in word and deed, that he could effectively manage his dual responsibilities to the MHP and to the CMCP. His decision not to recruit the Medical Director to serve in the

MHP was more problematic, due to its personal nature.
His decision was based upon an opinion that:

> The Medical Director lacked clinical and program-
> matic competence, was politically too convention-
> al, was a poor teacher and generally was an up-
> tight person I would not inflict on trainees and
> other staff. I handled his interest in the MHP
> by shrugging and not answering his comments
> about participating in the MHP.

The Medical Director's ire over being excluded from the
MHP was exacerbated when another psychiatrist from the
CMCP was selected to provide consultative services to the
MHP. Since the consultant was also Caucasian (as was
every clinician at the CMCP) the Medical Director could
justifiably refute Mr. Leavitt's contention that he was
not extensively drawing on CMCP manpower for the MHP
because he was attempting to effect a proper ethnic balance at the college. The interpersonal, rather *sub rosa*
antipathy which existed between these two men came to
play a pivotal role in the MHP, about which there will be
further elaboration later in this book.

In describing the *modus operandi* between the
WCMHS and himself, Mr. Leavitt states the following:

> I was well known and trusted at the WCMHS. I
> had served as one of the founding members of
> their Board of Directors and had been a close
> professional colleague of the WCMHS Executive
> Director for some time. That agency, of course,
> is a community-oriented one, so the MHP was a
> program it could easily support and it cost
> them, relatively speaking, very little money.
> On the basis of their explicit trust in me and

> because the program was rather peripheral, fiscally and geographically, I could work as an effective broker, bringing people together and insuring that everyone benefited.

The highly personalized and informal understandings and agreements which flowed between Mr. Leavitt and the WCMHS were of enormous benefit to the MHP, since more formalized procedures would have unnecessarily delayed the formation of the MHP. By, more or less, unilaterally designing the administrative structure and selecting the clinical staff for the MHP, Mr. Leavitt avoided many potential bureaucratic impediments. Conversely, the circumvention of formalized bureaucratic procedures laid the groundwork for growth of a dangerous administrative vacuum in the event that Mr. Leavitt withdrew from the MHP. How such an actual eventuality affected the MHP will be included in a later discussion.

In spelling out his thoughts about the City College administrative staff with whom he originally dealt, Mr. Leavitt comments that he found:

> They were slick, slightly devious and psychopathic-like. They were a smart group which knew how to avoid or suppress student dissidence. They maintained a trade-school attitude which meant that students should not expect more than they had already received in high school with respect to social and health programs.

The college administration, although it assiduously organized an ever-widening range of educational programs

for the poor and disadvantaged, took particular pride in
"turning out persons who were basically apolitical, technically competent and quite satisfied with the *status
quo*" (Mr. Leavitt, 1977).

In explaining why such an authoritarian administration would accept a mental health service on its prem-
ises, particularly since mental health programs are often
legitimately viewed as genuine threats to the *status quo*,
Mr. Leavitt remarks, "Most likely they felt that psychological services could neutralize student grievances and
deal most effectively with crazy and militant students."

Furthermore, the administrative staff of the college, most likely, erroneously concluded that:

> They could control us. That we had no protection
> from them. We cost them no money, except for the
> minor costs of rooms and supplies. Perhaps we
> could assist them fiscally by reducing the stu-
> dent drop-out rate (the college receives state
> reimbursement based on the size of enrollment),
> but in any case the college administration's
> expectations were that the MHP could never build
> a strong constituency which would fight for its
> continuance. (Mr. Leavitt, 1977)

In short, the agreement to allow the MHP on campus
was largely based upon the college administration's pre-
supposition (mistaken, as it turned out) that it possessed unilateral power to eliminate this psychological
experiment if it so wished. In no discernible respect
did any set of humanistic social values or sense of ide-

26

alism about the MHP emanate from the highest levels of the administration at that time.

Mr. Leavitt, then, navigated the MHP through a labyrinth of parallel governing agencies which were highly dissimilar in their programmatic priorities and social orientations, almost to the point of making their administrative governance of the MHP unintelligible. He chose, therefore, to assume an individualistic style of leadership which left him almost completely administratively unruled and unrulable during the earliest developmental phases of the MHP. This author enjoins the reader from construing such administrative leadership ("I did as I damned pleased") as either amoral or duplicitous professional conduct. On the contrary, at the time that the MHP was established in 1970, the very survival of this humanistic endeavor depended primarily upon this kind of Weberian charismatic leader who could skillfully convince, cajole, bestir and even repress (as in the case of the CMCP Medical Director) others. Nevertheless, it must be acknowledged that charismatic authority can eventually become maladaptive and, as in the case of the MHP, may leave an onerous legacy to a social organization. How such a legacy ultimately affected the MHP will be discussed in Chapters IV and V.

Weber offers the following characterization of the

27

charismatic leader which, to a considerable extent, corresponds with the self-characterization of Mr. Leavitt.

> The charismatic hero does not deduce his authority from codes and statutes, as is the case with the jurisdiction of office. The charismatic leader gains and maintains authority solely by proving his strength in life. Genuine charismatic domination therefore knows of no "formal" way of adjudication. Its "objective" law emanates concretely from the highly personal experience of heavenly grace and from the god-like strength of the hero. Charismatic domination means a rejection of all ties to any external order in favor of the exclusive glorification of the genuine mentality of the prophet and hero. Hence, its attitude is revolutionary and transvalues everything; it makes a sovereign break with all traditional or rational norms: "It is written, but I say unto you." (Weber, 1976, p. 250)

By proving his "strength in life," Mr. Leavitt sliced through a vast network of bureaucratic red-tape. By being beholden primarily to himself he obviated the possibility that the governing organizations would exercise their official prerogatives by perhaps unduly shaping, interfering with or usurping his decision-making powers. Charismatic leadership undoubtedly served him and the MHP well, and, as Weber suggests, was truly revolutionary in nature.

Weber also elucidates the pitfalls of charismatic leadership, many of which will become evident later in this history.

> By its very nature, the existence of charismatic authority is specifically unstable. The holder may forego his charisma; he may prove to his fol-

28

lowers that "virtue is gone out of him." It is then that his mission is extinguished, and hope waits and searches for a new holder of charisma. The charismatic holder is deserted by his following, however (only) because pure charisma does not know any "legitimacy" other than that flowing from personal strength, that is, one which is constantly being proved.
(Weber, 1976, p. 248)

The later history of the MHP will reveal what specific instabilities, disillusionments and desertions resulted from the charismatic foundation which maintained the MHP in its formative years.

II

THE MENTAL HEALTH PROGRAM

Rationales for College Mental Health Services

In 1970, there was a paucity of information regarding the health status of City College students. The
college administration, authoritarian in outlook, was
not on the lookout for covert or subtle psychological
dilemmas of students. In one of the earliest meetings
in 1969 with the then President and Vice President (in
1969 there was no position of Chancellor-Superintendent)
Mr. Leavitt alluded to the findings of Dana Farnsworth.

Farnsworth (Glasscote, 1973), using a variety of
data at Harvard University (a relatively low-risk student
population), estimated that for every 10,000 students:

> 1,000 will have emotional conflicts of sufficient
> severity to warrant professional help.
>
> 300 to 400 will have feelings of depression se-
> vere enough to impair their efficiency.
>
> 100 to 200 will be apathetic and unable to organ-
> ize their efforts -- "I can't make myself want
> to work."
>
> 20 to 50 will become ill enough to require
> treatment in a mental hospital.

5 to 20 will attempt suicide, of whom one or more will succeed. (p. 26)

Recognition of the debilitating emotional stress of many students and the need for colleges and universities to take affirmative measures to cope effectively with that stress was expressed by President William A. Stearns of Amherst over 100 years ago:

> The breaking down of the health of students, especially in the spring of the year, which is exceedingly common, involving the necessity of leaving college in many instances, and crippling the energies and destroying the prospects of not a few who remain is in my opinion wholly unnecessary if proper measures could be taken to prevent it. (Stearns, 1869, p. 3)

Although the rationales commonly adduced in the advocacy of college mental health services tend to dramatize the psychopathology and morbidity of students, such one-sided championing is rather outmoded and potentially insulting to students. As indicated by Binger (1961), the fact that about 10 per cent of students may require professional assistance during their college careers, is not an indication that "those who seek help are necessarily sicker than those who do not. They may simply recognize and acknowledge difficulties which others try to deny" (Binger, 1961, p. 184).

Certainly a campus mental health service must be amply prepared to respond to students who suffer from severe psychological stresses and vicissitudes. It must be a dependable and useful refuge for those students who have chronic personality disorders, including those of the psychotic variety. On the other hand, a mental health service should not be instituted on the basis of a spurious and self-defeating notion that it is a facility which will be beneficial solely or even primarily to "sick" students. To identify the utility of a psychological service in such a tendentious manner might seriously discourage the utilization of such a program even by those students who truly suffer from serious psychiatric disorders and would certainly dissuade the more well functioning students who periodically require help with transient psychological difficulties.

The experience of higher education has been recognized by Freedman as one which has the potential for animating an

> appreciation of the complexity of people and social events, openness to new experiences, flexibility in thinking, compassion in judgment of people, and the like. These changes are large in some students, small in others. But few go through college without acquiring at least a tinge of this liberalization and the social consequences of such changes are enormous. (Freedman, 1967, P. 6)

Jade Snow Wong, an alumna of City College of San Francisco, in her poignant autobiographical book, *Fifth Chinese Daughter*, states in personal terms how two years of college critically reorganized her personality.

> Hand in hand with a growing awareness of herself
> and her personal world (Wong writes of herself
> in the third person), there was developing in her
> an awareness of and a feeling for the larger world
> beyond the familiar pattern. The two years had
> made her a little wiser in the ways of the world,
> a little more realistic, less of a dreamer, and
> she hoped more of a personality. (Wong, 1945,
> p. 132)

If the experience of learning in college is dynamic and serves as a catalyst to further personal growth and understanding for many students, a college mental health program can legitimately be predicated upon the rightful aspirations of such students to further experiment and self-discover, in a credible psychological milieu within the educational institution itself. Consistent with the conviction that a college mental health service is a natural resource for the psychological and intellectual liberalization of students are the following humanistic propositions about education and youth:

1. Each individual is different from every other one and these differences are desirable and should be fostered.

2. Each individual has potential which is not used; in fact, the mind has unfathomed possibilities and the limits of human potentiality are still unknown.

3. Abilities must be developed and used if the individual is to be psychologically healthy.

4. In the development of attitudes and abilities, interaction will always be between organism and environment, though each individual must develop according to his own design.

34

5. Each individual seeks to learn about himself and others in the course of his development, although this search may not always be a conscious one.

6. The more highly developed individuals are characterized by a high degree of differentiation (complexity) and a high degree of integration (wholeness).

7. The individual is all of a piece and functions as a unit. Intellect, feeling, emotion and action can be separated conceptually yet no one of these functions independently of the others.

8. The values and purposes of the individual (the development of character) are central to education. Nothing is learned until it is integrated with the purposes of the individual. (Drews, 1966, pp. 108-109)

In contrast to the above-mentioned propositions, the highest levels of the City College administration, in 1970, maintained an adherence to a largely authoritarian set of ideals. The administration repeatedly and lavishly placed great value upon such human traits as conformity, manneriness, gratitude, obedience, loyalty, unaggressiveness, cleanliness, and moral certitude. The antithetical values held by those serving in the MHP and those serving in the highest levels of the college administration in 1970 were a made-to-order formula for the many struggles and clashes which often threatened the very survival of the MHP throughout its history.

With the advent of the MHP several service priorities were established:

1. To deal rapidly and effectively with basically well functioning students in psychological crisis.

2. To refer those students in need of services that were not available at the college to other community resources.

3. To provide supportive services on an ongoing basis to some severely disturbed students needing such assistance.

4. To help students learn as much as possible about the maintenance of mental health and the minimization of emotional stress.

5. To make consultative services readily available to all college personnel, with respect to their concerns about the mental health needs of students.

In order to implement these service goals the following guidelines and policies were adopted: there would be no charge for services and intake was to be entirely voluntary, i.e., no student would be seen against his or her wishes. All information was to be held in strict confidence within the SHS, kept separate from all other student records. The importance of the preservation of confidentiality applied also to the question of whether or not a particular student had

36

come to clinic at all. The program would maintain an "open" intake -- seeing any regularly enrolled student who applied as soon as possible after application. Waiting periods and waiting lists would be kept to a minimum.

The general goal of psychological services was to promote personal growth by giving students an opportunity to explore problems which interfered with studies, work, and relationships with family and friends. Those clinical staff recruited to the program were specially sought for their proven skills, sensitivity and experience in handling acute problems. The ethnic composition of the staff would approximate the composition of the multiethnic student body (Carey & Leavitt, 1971). This practice would hopefully encourage minority students to utilize the psychological services in numbers proportionate to their percentages in the student body as a whole.

The mainstay of the program was to be short-term crisis-oriented services to insure the availability of immediate appointments for a maximum number of students.

> The long wait for treatment insures that only the most regressed and dependent people remain, since those with any ego strengths have made arrangements for therapy elsewhere, a process of case selection which almost guarantees therapeutic failure. (Lewin, 1970, p. 4)

I have suggested that,

> A valid basis for providing short-term psycho-
> therapeutic services is the indisputable fact
> that the foremost concern of the vast majority
> of prospective psychiatric patients is immedi-
> ate psychological relief and not basic personal-
> ity transformation. It is manifestly illogical
> and self-defeating to gear a therapeutic philoso-
> phy and set of clinical techniques primarily to
> the luxuries of long-term contact when the pre-
> ponderance of psychiatric patients are more a-
> menable to short-term modalities. (Amada, 1977,
> p. 105)

Although it was expected that most students would
receive individual psychotherapeutic services, provisions were made for group therapy as well. Group services were developed to assist students whose problems
were largely in the area of interpersonal relations.
Group members were to be encouraged to express feelings,
share insights, and test perceptions with their college
peers. A prediction made at the time when groups were
first organized, which was later borne out by the empirical observations of group leaders, was that a significant number of students would derive far more benefit
from group psychotherapy than they could possibly gain
from a more socially limited one-to-one relationship with
a therapist.

In writing about college students in particular,
Millard Ryker (1970) states:

> For a peer-oriented student in the throes of a
> situational crisis, where better to find the

support so necessary to resolve it successfully than in a warm, concerned group of peers . . . peers with whom most college students are primarily concerned, are present so he may test his interactional skills and shape his identity. Authority figures, in the persons of the therapists, are also present to lend sanction to these activities and to provide a testing ground for relations with authority figures in the student's true environment, such as parents or college professors and deans. In summary, then, a group could provide support for the members as they meet the various inevitable crises of college life and also provide an atmosphere in which they may shape and test their emerging identities. (Ryker, 1970, p. 296)

In order to maximize the effectiveness of groups, careful screening of applicants would be undertaken. This procedure would, hopefully, result in exclusion of students who either lacked adequate motivation or were potentially disruptive.

In addition to direct individual and group psychotherapeutic services, plans were formulated to provide consultation to all college personnel who requested information or advice about dealing with student mental health needs. Faculty members would be able to utilize information and suggestions on how to modify teaching techniques, for example. Perhaps, through such consultation, the need for formal psychotherapy, would be averted. Also, by helping instructors with students whose emotional problems were disruptive or time-consuming tasks, instructors would be able to tend to their academic responsibilities without undue interference.

39

There was immediate recognition by the MHP administrators that education would be important in removing the stigma often attached to psychotherapeutic clients. Thus, consultation services were designed to enable students who received mental health services, if they were at all identifiable, to be treated no differently from other students. To this end, staff members would seek invitations to classrooms and student organizations to introduce the MHP in its most palatable form, i.e., as a service oriented to the psychological strengths and well being of students.

Because the clinical mainstay of the program was to be short-term psychotherapy, provisions for inter-agency referrals were immediately instituted. Staff of the MHP would rely upon resource material and their own expertise in making referrals to, for example, social service agencies, family service agencies, psychiatric clinics, public-welfare agencies, and private practitioners.

Particular discretion would be used in implementing such referrals as they are sometimes apt to be a delicate process with unpredictable effects upon the student. As Farnsworth (1957) suggests, in order to carry out a satisfactory referral a therapist must be cognizant of the potential element of disgrace, hopelessness or rejection which the student may attach to the experience of being sent from one person to another. Thus, if therapeutic termination and referral become absolutely necessary, there would be unfaltering attempts to "convey to the student the fact that the relationship could not continue for practical reasons and that the student could better meet his or her needs elsewhere" (Amada & Swartz, 1972, p. 533). It would be made clear that referrals were made for objective reasons and were related to the needs of the other students and not because the student's problems were unwelcome or because he or she had done anything to offend the therapist. Also, it was deemed helpful to inform the student of the limitations on service at the beginning of therapy.

The innovativeness and boldness of the MHP's services and philosophical orientation become clearer when we examine the elements of the City College Counseling Department which received unanimous endorsement from the college administration until recently. The Counseling Department, which was established in 1942, assigns professionally trained counselors to 400-500 students per semester. Academic counseling primarily deals with current information concerning course requirements, transfer procedures, and other academic areas of concern. Since for many years these consid-

erations constituted the totality of the college administration's commitment to "counseling" students, is it
any wonder that an intense controversy constantly raged
between the MHP and the college administration over the
nature, goals and legitimacy of the services of the
MHP?

In a book ironically entitled *Planning and Developing Innovative Community Colleges,* the authors refer
to an ostensibly innovative counseling service in a community college near Chicago which hires counselors to
work with students on a 300:1 ratio and where "good mental hygiene will be stressed and *serious problems will
be referred"* (1973; emphasis added). The same authors
concede that in certain "severe cases of maladjustment,"
students are often reluctant to seek help outside the
college. In suggesting a solution to this dilemma, they
call upon Twyman Jones, who recommends, "Some colleges
may wish to consider the possibility of including one or
more doctoral-level clinical or counseling psychologists
as members of their counseling staffs" (Jones, 1973,
p. 220). The multiple qualifiers, "some," "many," "consider," "possibility," the rigid requirement of doctoral-
level practitioners and the general treatment in the
above-quoted statement of psychotherapy as a peripheral
rather than integral component of a counseling service,

42

may give the reader a clearer impression of how terribly
cautious even "progressive" community college leaders
become in recommending mental health services to wary
college administrations.

III

THE MENTAL HEALTH PROGRAM, 1970-72

The Training Program

In the Fall of 1970, a psychological training program was integrated into the MHP. In order to adequately reflect and respond to a highly multiethnic student population, a policy decision was made by the MHP administrators that at least half of the staff members would be from ethnic minorities. This decision was based upon ethical considerations, upon a view that minority students would more readily trust a multiethnic staff, and upon a conviction that minority staff would provide a unique perspective in the development of psychological services for minority students.

Trainees, rather than additional experienced clinicians, were recruited for two reasons primarily: (1) to augment salaried staff and clinical services without incurring weighty financial costs (trainees received modest stipends from the program grant), and (2) to infuse the program with a youthful, vigorous group of persons who would seek to effect positive social change.

45

During the process of recruiting minority trainees for the MHP it was discovered that other Bay Area
mental health agencies had been actively seeking to recruit minority graduate students also. Frequently,
however, other agencies would not be able to fulfill the
promises they made to prospective trainees that they
would be afforded extensive opportunities to work with
minority populations; the MHP was one such fertile opportunity.

Because the MHP was relatively new and unstruc-
tured administratively, trainees were in an advantageous position to plan and determine many of their own
responsibilities and assignments. Some of these responsibilities included planning the training conferences,
selecting conference leaders and supervisors, and recruiting future trainees to the MHP. Aside from the
more complicated administrative and consultative responsibilities which were largely shouldered by senior
staff, trainees assumed a large share of the direct
service workload. This provided them with a sense of
pride and achievement as well as a stimulating learning experience.

Although long-term psychotherapy was de-empha-
sized, trainees were encouraged, as an additional learning experience, to offer long-term therapy to several

46

students each semester. Trainees were also aided in organizing and implementing psychotherapy groups which sometimes ran for entire semesters. Trainees were also expected to develop other activities and services such as assisting student organizations in their efforts to legitimate and stabilize their particular activities on the campus.

Specific examples of trainee assignments include the following:

(a) One trainee, a psychiatric nurse who had formerly been a fashion model, worked with faculty in the women's physical education department which offered special classes for obese women. These women met regularly with the trainee with an initial emphasis placed upon grooming and posture. Gradually the sessions began to focus upon the physiological aspects of obesity, and eventually the psychological factors underlying obesity were addressed. As certain of the group members achieved success in weight reduction, important discussions took place involving the student's changing sense of self-image.

(b) Two Black trainees worked intensively in trying to help the Black Students Union become a more effective organization. Trainees worked with the BSU in generating new membership and in locating and pro-

47

curing a permanent office on campus. This office soon
became a social center for a significant number of
Black students who used it when they were not attending
classes.

The MHP devised a unique approach to the supervision of minority trainees. Through the use of a dual
supervisory system each minority trainee had a clinical
supervisor, usually from a different ethnic background,
and a second supervisor from the trainee's own ethnic
background. The availability of an ethnic consultant
offered many advantages. The ethnic consultant could be
a resource for certain cultural knowledge and also serve
as a role model for the trainee. In addition, the ethnic
consultant could help trainees who tended to over-identi-
fy with ethnic clients; through careful assessment of
the clinical material the ethnic consultant could con-
front distortions resulting from ethnocentrism, when
they arose.

The minority consultant often served as an effective mediator for the trainee and clinical supervisor during times of stress or conflict. For example, a
minority trainee who was dissatisfied with his first
evaluation threatened to appeal the matter to the administration of his graduate school. As his clinical supervisor and author of his evaluation, I considered his

48

reaction exaggerated and unfair. After reaching an impasse in dealing with the trainee, I referred the matter to the ethnic consultant for further review. The ethnic consultant was invaluable in clarifying the areas of conflict and in recommending a means of resolution.

In addition to individual supervision, trainees attended weekly conferences with senior staff. Those conferences would focus upon the knowledge requisite for undertaking crisis intervention. The agenda of these conferences might include case presentations, guest lectures, or occasional discussions of complex administrative matters.

The trainees selected for the MHP had been recruited primarily from the San Francisco State University Graduate Schools of Social Welfare and Rehabilitation Counseling and the University of California, Berkeley, Graduate School of Social Welfare. Initially, psychiatric residents from the Department of Psychiatry at Mt. Zion Hospital and interns from a refresher training program at the CMCP were also recruited.

In the first year of the training program, seven trainees were first-year graduate students; five members of this group had considerable relevant clinical

experience before they entered the program. Two of the
seven were registered nurses who were particularly interested in acquiring psychotherapeutic skills in a college setting. In addition to the seven there were also
four so-called senior trainees. Two were third-year psychiatric residents, one was a psychiatric social worker
in his fourth year of graduate clinical training, and
one was a second-year student in vocational rehabilitation counseling with a great deal of prior experience.
Three of the eleven trainees were foreign born and four
were community college graduates. Ethnically, three
were Black, three were Chinese, one was Latin and four
were White.

Although the trainees came with no expectations
of salary for their work, financial stipends became a-
vailable during the course of the first semester of
their work. Since most of the trainees were themselves
from low-income backgrounds and were forced to work
part-time while attending graduate school, these stipends were a genuine boon to their service in the MHP.
The stipends enhanced their morale by giving tangible
indication of respect for their work.

The use of trainees held many advantages for the
MHP. Trainees brought fresh perspectives and new ideas
for programmatic improvement. Minority trainees were

often more adept and comfortable in establishing rapport with minority students than more experienced White staff. Also minority trainees served as positive role models for students who were aspiring to be successful academically and vocationally.

An important footnote to this training program was the fact that all six trainees who completed their training in the Spring of 1971 took paid positions where their primary responsibilities were to provide services in ethnic and poverty ghettos. The experience for trainees and senior staff alike was exhilarating, but in order to carry out such an innovative program, "one must be prepared to go outside the formal bureaucratic and administrative channels," according to Leavitt and Curry (1973).

The training program quickly became a thorn in the administrative hides of two of the organizations to which the MHP was directly accountable: CMCP and the college administration. As indicated earlier, the antipathy for the newly organized training program on the part of CMCP primarily stemmed from the exclusion of its medical director from participation in the MHP. The objections of the college administration were more complex and more difficult to define.

The college administration reprehended the MHP

training program for "excessively diverting MHP senior staff energies and time from more essential activities," i.e., direct clinical services to students. This contention was soundly rebutted by the MHP staff, which readily documented the fact that each hour of training was effectively converted into at least three to five hours of service provided by trainees to students, an argument to which the college administration remained fixedly oblivious.

Although there were limited attempts elsewhere in the college (i.e., the Counseling Department) to provide training experiences for graduate students, no other college program regarded and treated its trainees as quite so essential to its operation. The time, effort and commitment extended by and to trainees, although kept within reasonable limits, had the effect of causing jealousy and disgruntlement among the college administration which, in the tradition of authoritarianism, measured the value of the MHP according to how loyally and exclusively committed its administrators were to their administrative superiors at the college.

The college administration conveyed its authoritarian attitude toward the trainees in a countless number of revealing incidents. A departmental policy governing dresswear in physical education courses led to a serious altercation between a White instructor and a Chicano student. The instructor called the Dean of Students to complain about the student and to request that disciplinary action be taken. The Dean of Students, without first alerting me to the matter, advised the instructor to apprise me of the incident and to gain my assistance. After hearing the instructor's description of the problem, I asked him how I might be of help. He stated that he really did not think the matter required psychological intervention, but he called me only because he was directed to do so by the Dean.

I concurred with the instructor's viewpoint that the matter probably required administrative rather than psychological measures. Although I did not fully share my opinions of the situation with him, it seemed to me that the conflict resulted primarily from enforcement of unreasonably rigid dresswear requirements and a degree of ethnic prejudice on the part of the instructor (later manifested in the form of contemptuous remarks about the student's linguistic deficiencies).

The instructor indicated that he would refer the matter back to the Dean of Students. Moments later, the Dean of Students called to inform me that I had not properly handled the request for help. I asked him to clarify his criticism. He remarked that the student was psychologically disturbed and required "treatment." I responded by stating that, although I had had no direct contact with the student, it was my impression that he had justifiable cause for being disturbed with the instructor. I added that perhaps an evaluation of the instructor's policies and professional conduct might be more appropriate. I again was informed that I was being remiss in my duties.

I then asked what specific measures he would recommend. He said he wanted me to send Ms. G., a Spanish-speaking, Chicana trainee to seek out the student. He contended that her linguistic and cultural affinity with the irate student would neutralize his recalcitrance. I responded by reminding him that Ms. G. was relatively inexperienced and physically diminutive. I opined that, as a mental health staff member, her unsolicited attempt to assist the student might be construed as intrusive and insulting. Perhaps she might inadvertently worsen a bad situation and, thereby, endanger herself. He replied that the college was doing the trainees a favor by providing them with a field placement and that they owed the college certain personal sacrifices. I told him that I would not subject students or trainees to situations which were fraught with so many hazards. The discussion ended at that point, in an uncomfortable stalemate.

Incidentally, I believe my manner of responding to the Dean's request is a refutation of Szasz's dogmatic contention that college psychotherapists assume that students who break social customs or regulations "are mentally ill until proven otherwise," and that the task of the psychotherapist is "to divide these quasi-criminals into two groups: those who break rules 'from sheer perversity' and those who do so because of "illness.'"

A second reason which was inferred for the college administration's reservations about the training program was the fact that the trainees, by their sheer numbers, enlarged the MHP to dimensions which threatened the college administration's confidence that it could securely control the direction and influence of the MHP. Since, as indicated earlier, the college administration "bought" the MHP because it was perceived as wieldy, it regarded the increase in the number of MHP staff, albeit of trainee status, as a potential formidable force with which it might have trouble reckoning.

A third reason the college administration looked askance at the training program was the fact that the trainees themselves were preponderantly an "outside," Third World, unconventionally dressed (for the college) and humanistically oriented group. The trainees, as a group, were singular within the college system, in their ethnic composition and public manner. Their informality, political orientation (liberal to radical), spontaneity and innovativeness were qualities which were tradition- ally distrusted by the authoritarian college administra- tors. It was no surprise that the college administration would object to having such a group gain credibility on the campus. Since the college administration's actual objections to the trainees were perhaps only partly con- sciously held and since these objections could not una- bashedly be articulated publicly, the misgivings about the training program were repeatedly translated into al- legations that the MHP senior staff were diverting their time and energies into "wasteful" training activities.

The great value which was placed, by the college administration, upon exclusive ingroup loyalty to admin- istrative superiors, upon the controllability of admin- istrative inferiors, and upon conventionality of behav- ior and attitude became very perceptible as the MHP training program went into full swing. Such preoccupa- tions with and pride in ingroup loyalty, conventionality and dominance-submission have been referred to by Adorno, *et al*. (1964) in describing salient characteristics of the authoritarian personality.

The Authoritarian Personality

    a. Conventionalism. Rigid adherence to conventional, middle class values.

    b. Authoritarian submission. Submissive, uncritical attitude toward idealized moral authorities of the ingroup.

    c. Authoritarian aggression. Tendency to be on the lookout for, and to condemn, reject, and punish people who violate conventional values.

    d. Power and "toughness." Preoccupation with the dominance-submission, strong-weak, leader-follower dimension. (Adorno, *et al.*, 1964, p. 228)

R. Jean Hills (1968), in discussing educational organizations, considers the authoritarian tendencies of such bureaucracies to develop a zealous adherence to "pattern-maintenance." She suggests that such institutions have particular concern with the integrity of their own value system. At times the educational organization may seek to maintain its integrity at the expense of adaptation, goal-attainment and integration.

> Hence, organizational goals, adaptive procedures, and the procedures by which the organization is integrated with other units must be interpreted in terms of their meaning for the integrity of the value system. From this there follows a tendency to dichotomize situations into categories such as, "good-bad," "right-wrong," etc. The organization with (authoritarian) pattern-maintenance primacy is likely to be uncompromisingly idealistic, and to define situations in black and white terms as either appropriate for the organization, or totally inappropriate. Any compromise of this position made in the interest of adaptation, goal-attainment, or integration, tends to be viewed as an expediency.

(Hills, 1968, p. 99)

The introduction of the training program into the MHP exacerbated relations between the MHP and the college administration. The college administration, doggedly seeking to maintain its own (authoritarian) value system, regarded the training program as "wrong" and "bad" and most certainly inappropriate for the educational institution.

The Student Health Advisory Board

The largest and most immediately accessible source of manpower on a college campus is the student body itself. Students can provide a wealth of talent, creativity and energy if effective ways can be found to involve them in surveying health needs and in the planning and staffing of vitally needed health services. The most likely sources of potential health personnel among the student body are military veterans who have worked as corpsmen; health professionals who received their training in foreign countries and have encountered problems in working in the United States due to language or licensing difficulties; psychiatric technicians and licensed vocational nurses returning for additional academic training; and older students with valuable work experience.

58

If students with health knowledge and interests can be enlisted to provide appropriate services under the supervision of health professionals, enormous benefits can accrue. Limited budgets can be stretched; students who provide services can be paid stipends for their work and/or given academic credit for their services; with student participation in planning and delivering health services these programs can become more relevant, and, in the case of outreach services, hard-to-reach students frequently can be better identified and reached by their peers.

In July, 1970 a Special Opportunity Grant was received by the City College Student Health Service to plan a comprehensive student multiservice center. Because the plan was innovative and unique, it was considered to be a potential model for community colleges throughout the nation. Although the funds for this project were not forthcoming until July, 1970, staff members of the Student Health Service, including the MHP Administrative Director (Mr. Leavitt) and the PHN, had already engaged in a limited way in planning such a program (Leavitt & Carey, 1970).

The Student Health Advisory Board (SHAB) was organized by the planning staff as an important vehicle with which to ascertain and meet student health needs.

Students were requested to conceive of an ideal student health service and advised to disregard realistic barriers which such a program might encounter.

The process of organizing the SHAB began when the health planner contacted all student organizations and asked them to send representatives to a mass meeting. Individual students were also invited to attend this meeting. Planners made a conscientious attempt to invite minority students to attend this meeting in significant numbers: seats were reserved on the SHAB for each ethnic group. The process of selection to the SHAB was predicated upon a firm resolution to insure that the SHAB would be balanced and truly representative of the entire student body. An essential incentive to the SHAB members was the hourly wages which they received for their work from the planning grant funds.

During the first (mass) meeting of the SHAB an agenda was set upon to deal with health needs and priorities, with staff discussing existing services as well as ideas and projections for the future. In the estimation of the SHAB members themselves, the project began "beautifully" (Swartz, 1972).

An immediate administrative conundrum developed over the allocation of power and funds. Although students were hired as consultants to this project, with an

60

equal voice to the health professionals, they were paid far less than the latter. Although such inequities fostered resentment and distrust, students decided to continue participating in the project, despite apparent contradictions.

> A second fly in the ointment involved hiring procedures. Here too, students were legally responsible for 50% of the decision, in theory. When a few positions were to be filled a hiring committee was formed from the SHAB. With equal representation from the nonstudent staff, this committee proceeded to interview the applicants and nominees. At the recommendation of this committee, the positions were filled. Here's the catch: the entire committee should have come back to the SHAB with its recommendations so that the entire SHAB could make the actual decision. This should have been understood by both the students and the nonstudents, but apparently it wasn't. Again the students raised this question and continued to work on the planning grant despite this contradiction. (Swartz, 1972, P. 10)

Although the SHAB's grievances over its diminished decision-making power and the inequities in allocations of funds were entirely warranted, the SHAB members were not able to cogently trace or identify the actual source of their dissatisfaction: the authoritarianism of the college administration. The director of the planning project was the PHN who was directly accountable and subject to the authority of the college administration. Basically, the college administration tacitly, and sometimes explicitly, directed that students not be invested with decision-making authority relative to any college

61

program. Thus, the PHN was, at the outset of the planning project, completely obviated from sharing even her
limited authority with the SHAB. This point is admitted
in the final report by the health planners when they
suggest that students were pathetically enticed into
"competing with staff for power that even staff did not
possess."

How did the MHP deal with the college administration's attempts to emasculate the SHAB? In the latter
phase of the planning project, soon after assuming the
directorship of the MHP, I unqualifiedly disassociated
myself and the MHP from the authoritarian posture of
the college administration and the PHN. As an employee
of a community agency and, therefore, not exclusively
beholden to the college administration, I exploited my
considerable administrative latitude by sharing freely
with the SHAB my decision-making authority. This sharing
process affected three important tasks of the MHP: (1)
policy formulation; (2) program development; and (3)
hiring of MHP personnel.

An example of how the SHAB affected policy formulation is its contributions to developing a workable and
judicious policy of confidentiality for the MHP. By
recognizing flaws and pitfalls in the original statement
of confidentiality the SHAB was able to articulate a

new policy which has been operational ever since.

In contributing to program development the SHAB played a particularly vital role in the analyzing and eventual rescinding of a highly equivocal proposal to recruit manpower assistance from the Mission Mental Health Center. This proposal was considered for the "purpose of evaluating the feasibility of permanent assignment of Mission personnel at the college," and was belatedly discovered to be decidedly conditional (Leavitt, 1972). Through careful questioning, the SHAB learned from the Mission Mental Health Center Director that he intended to have his staff provide services at City College only to those students who were residents of the Mission district. The elitist and parochial orientation of such an administrative policy was quickly recognized and rebuffed by the SHAB, to the inestimable advantage of the MHP.

The SHAB's participation in the hiring procedures of prospective MHP personnel was thorough and painstaking. MHP administrators hired no new staff without review and approval from SHAB. The mutual respect and cooperation in this venture was gratifying to the MHP staff who were fully aware of the fact that their newly hired co-workers had passed the most difficult and perhaps most valid of all requirements for employment: the sanction of a genuine consumer group. (A substantial number of the SHAB's membership had received psychotherapeutic services in the MHP.)

The mutual appreciation and goodwill between the MHP and the SHAB were particularly impressive considering the SHAB's general findings regarding the process of working with the health professionals. In an otherwise scathing report of perceived widespread hypocrisy and complicity, the SHAB states.

> The relationship between the SHAB and the MHP staff has been and continues to be of mutual support and cooperation. The 50% student (consumer) control has been implemented into the MHP and has their full endorsement. (Swartz, 1972, p. 11)

The joint efforts of the SHAB and the MHP culminated in highly favorable newspaper publicity which provided both groups with much deserved recognition for their daring and innovativeness. *The San Francisco Chronicle* printed a three column article which opened with the spirited assertion:

> There has been a lot of talk recently about consumer control of health services. But the students at City College have done more than just talk -- they've taken over. And what they are now controlling is probably the most complete and most innovative mental health service at any junior college in the country. (Swartz, 1972, p. 13)

The San Francisco Chronicle article and past cooperative ventures between the SHAB and the MHP were fillips to the college administration to discourage and disparage the relationship between these two groups. Thus, in meeting with the Dean of Students (whose office was administratively directly responsible for overseeing the MHP), I was "reminded" that I basically had no administrative authority to share with students. The Dean described the sharing of decision-making between the SHAB and the MHP as a sham. Although there was every indication that all proceedings between the SHAB and the MHP were highly substantive, they were depicted as a kind of window-dressing of participatory democracy. Those students who had raised concerns over contradictions and inconsistencies in the planning project were referred to in the most derogatory terms, i.e., "paranoics," "psychopaths," "delinquents," etc.

Naturally, by defending its activities with the SHAB, the MHP staff anticipated that the college administration would regard the MHP with even greater suspicion. By not wavering from its strongly humanistic stance that students have the unassailable right to decision-making powers which affect their daily lives, the MHP placed itself in further opposition to and jeopardy with the college administration.

As a representative of the authoritarian college

administration, the Dean of Students was engaging in an autocratic mode of behavior common to authoritarian organizations. As pointed out by Rensis Likert (1959),

> The tighter the control in an organization, in the sense that decisions are made at the top and orders flow down, the greater tends to be the hostility between subordinates. In autocratic organizations, subordinates fight for power and status. (p. 196)

Functionaries, such as the Dean of Students, who determinedly conform to and represent the values of authoritarian or traditionalist administrations tend to view their organizations as closed systems. By attempting to exclude the SHAB from decision-making participation, the Dean misperceived the MHP as a unit completely constrained by the authoritarian rules of the college administration. As a result, he was averse to acknowledging the reality that the MHP could work democratically with the SHAB because it enjoyed strong support toward achieving that goal from its off-campus community sponsor, the Westside Community Mental Health Services.

> Traditionalists -- those who equate official command with power -- also tend to see organizations as closed systems. They seem to assume that organizations are antiseptically clean of influences from outside. As a consequence there is relatively little attention paid to the manner in which organizations adapt internal power alignments to external influences. (Pfiffner & Sherwood, 1964, p. 334)

The Dean's proclivity to deem the SHAB a group of

"psychopaths, paranoics and delinquents" can be understood as the authoritarian personality's disposition to
turn his aggression against outgroups (the SHAB and the
MHP). He must do so because he is psychologically unable to attack ingroup authorities, i.e., his own Chancellor-Superintendent, rather than because of intellectual confusion regarding the source of his frustration.
This theory (of psychological displacement) helps to explain why the aggression is so regularly justified in
moralistic terms, why it can become so violent and lose
all connection with the stimulus which originally set it
off (Adorno, *et al.*, 1964).

In addition to displacing his aggressions, the
authoritarian personality is projecting his own unacceptable impulses onto other individuals and groups who are
then rejected (Adorno, 1964). In effect, he is saying,
as the Dean did when he defined the SHAB as a group of
delinquents, "I am not bad and deserving of punishment,
they are."

In sum, the relationship between the SHAB members
and the MHP staff was an additional alliance which
strained relations between the MHP and the college administration. Yet the MHP staff unanimously agreed that
the resultant estrangement between the college administration and the MHP was a necessary and worthwhile price

67

to pay for fulfilling a humanistic principle.

The Relationship of the Public Health Nurse to the MHP

The relationship of the PHN (who was both Coordinator of Student Health Services and Director of the Planning Grant) to the MHP was pivotal to the future of the MHP. It was also a highly anomalous relationship. The MHP staff were officially employed by two community agencies, the CMCP and the WCMHS. The PHN was an employee of the community college district. The community college district designated the MHP staff as subordinate to the PHN who had responsibility for directing the entire Student Health Service. Yet the MHP was designated and perceived by the CMCP and the WCMHS as administratively co-equal with the PHN. These contradictory and conflicting perceptions and expectations of the college district and community agencies produced a continual state of contentiousness for ill-defined administrative power.

The PHN was "energetic, bright, efficient and a no bullshit person" (Mr. Leavitt, 1977). In displaying great determination and competence in establishing the MHP on the campus she assumed a strong proprietary attitude toward the MHP. In concurrence with the views and values of her college administrative superordinates, she gave her blessing to the MHP only to the extent that she could trust it to be a reasonably controllable and malleable sub-department of the Student Health Service.

The PHN's influence was particularly felt in the following general areas: (1) in her attempt to affect the psychotherapeutic orientation (psychodynamic) of the MHP, (2) in her efforts to undercut the growth of the MHP, (3) in her periodic usurpation of the MHP's roles and responsibilities toward other campus personnel and departments, and (4) in her practice of maligning and interfering with the relationship between the SHAB and the MHP.

The PHN frequently discredited the MHP's psychological orientation as too impractical and permissive. Although, or perhaps especially because, she had no extensive formal psychological training herself, she appraised complicated psychological problems in an impatient, undynamic and cynical manner. For example, the unconscious defensive mechanisms employed by students in therapy were invariably dismissed by the PHN as "game-playing" manipulations which required authoritative, "no-nonsense" measures, such as pointedly telling students that their machinations would simply not be tolerated.

The PHN's initiatives to undercut the growth of

69

the MHP will be discussed in detail later in this report. Suffice it to say at this point that, despite clear assurances from the college administration in 1969 that the college district would eventually underwrite the MHP (Conlan, 1969), the PHN, who was primarily responsible for the budgetary planning of all student health services, eschewed or discouraged the institution of permanent funding arrangements for the MHP.

The PHN repeatedly usurped responsibility for negotiations regarding campus services which have naturally been assumed by the MHP. For example, a group of exuberant and resourceful student mothers visited the MHP requesting information, advice and direction in establishing an on-campus child-care center. Staff of the MHP were highly favorable to and encouraging of the organization of such an acutely needed service. The student mothers left the initial visit heartened and eager to work cooperatively with the MHP. In a second, rather adventitious contact with the PHN, these students learned from her that their project proposal would get little backing from the Student Health Service. Because the students, understandably, could not distinguish between the MHP and the Student Health Service as a whole, the MHP was tarred with the same angry brush of the students who accused all Student Health staff of callousness and reactionariness.

The relationship between the PHN and the SHAB was particularly problematic and had potential for damaging the MHP's credibility with the student group. As director of the planning project, the PHN was responsible for the allocation and supervision of funds and for the performance evaluations of students. In a relatively short time, the PHN alienated large segments of the SHAB with her autocratic leadership.

In describing the PHN's mode of communication and leadership, the SHAB members alleged that an "attitude of secretiveness" prevailed. They go on to report:

> There was a major problem of developing a relationship whereby the staff (principally represented by the PHN) would be able to offer the board options rather than patronizing attitudes, i.e., manipulating the board to do what the staff wanted it to do. There seemed to be an oversensitivity on the part of the staff and students in this area. Some of the staff referred to it as paranoia. It might better be identified as a healthy fear of being used as a rubber stamp consumer organization. (Swartz, 1972, pp. 55-56)

By alienating and disillusioning the SHAB, the PHN produced two general problems for the MHP. The first, as has already been discussed, was the dilemma of determining how to work compatibly with two warring factions, without completely jettisoning the integrity of the MHP. Although no explicit assertions were vocalized at the time, the MHP gradually opted to strongly dissociate it-

71

self from the PHN by working democratically and independently with the SHAB.

The second problem was in deciding how to demonstrate effectively the MHP's positive regard for the SHAB as it interfaced with the campus and off-campus communities. This was a quandary caused by the PHN's frequent public charges that the SHAB was a "bunch of paranoics." Thus, the MHP staff were constantly required to contradict and explain such unfounded accusations in the college and city communities, in order not only to protect its own credibility with the SHAB, but as a means of providing the SHAB with some immunity from adverse community reactions to the charges.

The association between the PHN and the MHP was, therefore, anomalous and quite untenable. Despite the fact that the PHN was the administrative progenitrix and principal advocate of the MHP at one time, her authoritarian outlook and administrative practices immediately pitted her against the goals and aspirations of the MHP staff. While acknowledging that the MHP was becoming a more integral part of the Student Health Service, it was also necessary for the MHP staff to demonstrate the important respects in which the MHP was philosophically distinguishable and autonomous from the PHN. Steering such a delicate and hazardous course was a central concern of the administrators of the MHP.

What organizational ingredients were necessary in order for the MHP to deal effectively with the PHN's attempts to modify or subvert its goals? Likert (1959) highlights three organizational characteristics which are important to the task of resolving conflict.

    A.   They (effective organizations) possess the machinery to deal constructively with conflict. This machinery includes an organizational structure which facilitates constructive interaction between persons and between work groups.

    B.   The personnel of the organization are skilled in the processes of effective interaction and mutual influence. These include skills in leadership and membership roles, and in group building and group maintenance functions.

    C.   There is high confidence and trust among the members of the organization in each other. (Likert, 1959, pp. 204-205)

The capacity of the MHP to weather the conflicts with the college administration and the PHN was based primarily upon its humanistic ethos. Its humanistic orientation promoted the "organizational structure which facilitated constructive interaction" and the high trust among the members of the organization in each other," both of which gave the MHP enormous moral strength.

The PHN's authoritarian administrative patterns clashed with the humanistic strivings of the MHP. Although much of this conflict was obviously attributable to the authoritarian organizational structure of the college and to the personality of the PHN who was favorably disposed to that structure, the factor of professional training was also crucial in how differently reality was perceived and treated. The professional training which one receives in conventional nursing programs is decidedly different from that which one undergoes in pursuing a career in psychological services. Professional training often can have a direct and profound affect upon one's perception of reality.

> Differences in modes of perceiving reality spring from the value structures implicit in the trained outlooks associated with various technical specialties. For example, engineers do not look at problems in the same way that economists or artists do. All three types might agree on explicit goals and even possess the same information, yet disagree on what the organization ought to do because their modes of perceiving that information emphasized different aspects of the problem. (Downs, 1967, p. 50).

Thus, even if the PHN and the MHP staff had identical goals (which they most certainly did not), their differential perceptual "worlds," which were, to an extent, based upon disparate value-instilling professional training experiences, would likely leave both with highly divergent conclusions about what their organization ought to do. Since the PHN was officially in a position to impose her perceptions of reality upon the MHP, poten-

74

tially through administrative recommendations or fiats, the MHP staff had to devise a viable method of neutralizing her influence when it was considered deleterious to the MHP. As suggested earlier, the mechanism decided upon, primarily by the Administrative Director of the MHP, was to establish a *de facto* state of equality of authority between himself and the PHN. This contrivance surely rankled the PHN, not only for personal reasons, but because it was logically refutable in that it violated the Table of Organization of the college. Yet it was a workable departure from the rigidity of the authoritarian structure of the college since it had the unblushing support of one of the sponsoring community agencies, the Westside Community Mental Health Services (WCMHS).

An additional dimension to the conflict between the PHN and the MHP was the struggle over what Downs (1967) calls "territorial sensitivity." He rightly proclaims that every social agent

> is essentially a territorial imperialist to some extent. He seeks to expand the borders of his various zones in policy space, or at least to increase his degree of influence within each zone. Merely trying to maintain the *status quo* implies a desire to prevent significant changes in and around one's heartland. (Downs, 1967, p. 216)

Thus, whenever social agents interact, their individual

or group imperialisms are bound to create some conflicts between them.

The PHN, who was guarding a much cherished heartland (the Student Health Service) was inclined toward obstructionism in responding to the MHP, which was seeking to expand its territorial vistas and sovereignty. However, the fact that the territorial conflicts became as virulent as they eventually did, I believe, can be attributed largely to the fact that these disputes took place within the context of an authoritarian host institution which bred interminable hostilities among subordinates.

The Relationship Between the MHP Director and the Clinical Coordinator

The relationship between the MHP Administrative Director (Mr. Leavitt) and the Clinical Coordinator (me) was one of great mutual respect and complementariness of leadership styles. Mr. Leavitt was imaginative, had extensive clinical experience and possessed considerable charisma. His plans and hopes for the MHP were visionary and socially advanced. With imagination and foresight he managed to establish a pioneering mental health venture on the City College campus which was already regarded by many other community colleges in California as a leader in the state.

76

As he recalls his experience, bringing ethnically and professionally diverse people together to form a new and unique MHP was one of the great thrills of his professional career (Mr. Leavitt, 1977). In response to his intelligence and charismatic optimism the MHP staff maintained high morale and unity.

In planning the goals and services of the MHP, Mr. Leavitt, as mentioned earlier, was inclined to make many important administrative decisions unilaterally. As his assistant, I was appropriately delegated such administrative responsibilities as supervising graduate students, coordinating staff schedules and compiling and distributing statistical reports. I, however, did not extensively participate in the planning and consultation which took place between Mr. Leavitt and the college administration, the PHN, the SHAB, and the sponsoring agencies of the MHP. Because of limitations of time and due to Mr. Leavitt's individualistic style of leadership, I was excluded from crucial programmatic planning: an administrative hiatus which was to have important implications for the MHP.

The fact that the program was then reasonably stable and non-controversial gave me false assurance of an unproblematic future. More importantly, my gratitude to Mr. Leavitt for recruiting me into the MHP engendered

in me a rather unquestioning confidence in his directorship of the MHP. I placed in him an inordinate hope
that he would navigate the MHP through all storms.

Mr. Leavitt's independent and charismatic style
of leadership had particular bearing upon my later adminstrative dealings with the college administration,
the PHN and the MHP's sponsoring agencies. In his earliest negotiations with the college administration, Mr.
Leavitt exacted no clear-cut commitments regarding the
long-range continuance of the MHP, notwithstanding the
earlier-mentioned assurance by the college president
that college district funds might be forthcoming in
1971-72.

Rather than legitimately place the onus for funding the MHP upon the college administration, Mr. Leavitt
enlisted the SHAB to

> fund a program they were not at all sure they
> had planned. In spite of some misgivings, the
> SHAB began the enormous task of getting the
> campus to adopt the health fee. Later, several
> students on and off the Board objected to the
> fee, and this facilitated a closer examination
> of what was involved in the areas of student
> control of their own money and their own serv-
> ices. (Swartz, 1972, p. 55)

Furthermore,

> Meetings with a lawyer revealed that all money
> collected would have to go through a general fund,
> thereby making the (health) fee an unlikely pos-
> sibility. (Swartz, 1972, p. 55)

Not surprisingly, the SHAB became "disillusioned" with the fee.

The college administration also opposed the imposition of a health fee. Their reasoning was that a health fee might constitute an untrustworthy precedent for the institution of additional college fees and perhaps would even be the precursor of generally unpopular tuition costs. They understandably viewed the spectre of health fees and tuition costs as potential sources of student discontent and disruption. Although the college administration proferred no viable alternatives for the financial maintenance of the MHP, it would not advocate or countenance a student health fee.

Thus, in the face of student and college administration disaffection with a health fee, Mr. Leavitt was pursuing a futile fiscal goal. In so doing, he held objectives for the MHP which were discordant with my own.

I eventually became convinced that a student health fee was not only impractical, but objectionable in principle, considering the economic marginality of many City College students. Because the "demonstration" funding was due to expire at the end of the second year and a health fee was virtually unattainable, I decided that the permanence of the MHP depended upon its full integration with the community college district.

Two points about Mr. Leavitt are germane in relation to the issue of the student health fee. (1) Mr. Leavitt was not in the least insensitive to the financial hardships of City College students. He viewed the health fee as a regrettable financial sacrifice which students might be willing to incur in order to gain vastly improved medical and psychological services.

> This was a difficult decision (to institute a health fee) for all of us because so many of our students are desperately poor, and because this would be the first compulsory fee and could be a precedent for others. (Mr. Leavitt, letter to Executive Director, Zellerbach Family Fund)

(2) Mr. Leavitt did not deliberately mislead or deceive the SHAB. He did lack the prescience to adequately anticipate that a student health fee which could not legally be controlled by students would not be supported by students.

Although Mr. Leavitt and I were at variance over how best to effect a financially solvent program, our differences were neither overt not divisive. One reason for this was my own reticence to openly raise doubts about a health fee because, for a short time, that goal seemed within reach. A second reason we did not have open and candid disagreements was my own, quite unwarranted, perception of Mr. Leavitt as having superhuman qualities. Almost to the very end of his tenure in the

80

MHP in December, 1971, I harbored an illusory hope that this charismatic leader would produce the *deus ex machina* which would rescue the MHP from dissolution. I did not realize that charisma, by its very nature, is not "An 'institutional' and permanent structure, but rather, where its 'pure' type is at work, it is the very opposite of the institutionally permanent" (Weber, in Gerth & Mills, 1976, p. 248).

Mr. Leavitt was not a "pure" charismatic leader (he had vast intellectual and pragmatic skills also). Nevertheless, once his mission was extinguished, there were painful realities which had to be faced and re-solved. How these administrative realities were dealt with will be discussed in the next two chapters.

IV

THE MENTAL HEALTH PROGRAM, 1972-74

The Ascendancy of the Clinical Coordinator to the Position of Administrative Director

In January, 1972, Mr. Leavitt relinquished his directorship of the MHP in order to take a sabbatical leave from the CMCP. His parting words of advise to me were, "Take care of No. 1." He appointed me his successor as director of the MHP, to assume the authority and responsibilities which he had formerly held.

My first realization was that the funding which supported the MHP would expire in the summer of 1972. Thus, unless new sources of revenue were tapped, the MHP would terminate at the end of the Spring semester, 1972.

My first official act as the new Administrative Director was to contact the WCMHS in order to inquire about the readiness of that agency to continue its funding of the MHP. I was assured that the WCMHS would continue to match funds which were generated elsewhere, but that WCMHS would definitely not be the sole provider of subsidies. I then turned to the Zellerbach Family Fund, which had been the original benefactor of the MHP.

Zellerbach informed me that it would be willing to continue subsidizing the MHP, but that the share of program costs which it had formerly borne would be sharply reduced. Both Zellerbach and the WCMHS stressed the point with me that the Community College District had financial obligations to the MHP which it was not fulfilling.

Since I had had little direct experience in working with the college administration and absolutely no knowledge of the intricacies of raising funds from the Community College District, I questioned the Dean of Students about the procedures for submitting monetary requests. He referred me to the PHN who was responsible, he said, as Coordinator of the Student Health Service, for requesting fiscal allocations. I immediately requested and received a budget-request form from the PHN. At the time I thought it curious that she, as Coordinator of the Student Health Service, had not volunteered information or forms which might assist me in procuring financial assistance from the college.

I next learned that funding for new programs, such as the MHP, was maximized by the process of lobbying, particularly in the form of faculty testimonials. There had been a faculty health advisory board which met irregularly and which maintained a friendly posture toward the programs of the SHS. I contacted each member of

84

the board, most of whom I knew rather well through our past collaborations in helping students in their respective programs, asking that they support my request for college district funding of the MHP. Each member readily consented to speak in behalf of the MHP.

My next administrative step was to arrange a meeting with the faculty health advisory board and the college President. Throughout this meeting the faculty members expressed strong, affirmative statements about the MHP's contribution to the college and unanimously iterated their opinion that the college district should begin to underwrite the MHP. I was startled when, near the conclusion of this meeting, the President, somewhat apologetically I thought, asked if the MHP could "manage" with an allocation of $30,000. An important sidelight to these negotiations was the timely assistance provided by the Chairperson of the SHAB. Just prior to the decisive meeting with the President of the college, I met with the SHAB Chairperson. He inquired as to the size of the grant I would be requesting from the college. I told him I intended to ask for $30,000. He suggested that I request twice that amount since the President would almost automatically prune the initial request by one-half. I took his advice, which proved to be uncannily prophetic.

The combined funding of the Zellerbach Family Fund, the Community College District and the WCMHS fell short of the original grant by about $7,500, a deficit which would necessitate a retrenchment of staff positions and services.

Shortly before I had assumed the directorship of the MHP I had made, through my private psychotherapy practice, numerous positive contacts with a San Francisco family which was in virtual control of a local foundation: The Bothin Helping Fund. I called the family member who was the highest ranking officer of the Bothin Helping Fund in order to familiarize her with the MHP's fiscal plight and to determine the advisability of submitting a grant request to that foundation. She was sympathetic and encouraging.

Soon after submitting a grant request I received formal notification that Bothin Helping Fund was allocating $15,000 to the MHP, to cover a one- or two-year period. This last allocation fully restored those funds which were lost due to the reduction in the Zellerbach grant. The MHP was assured continuance for at least one more year. Despite college district funding, the organizational sponsorship would remain jointly with the WCMHS and the CMCP.

The swift and dramatic resurgence of the MHP from

a financially moribund organization to a college-subsidized clinic with reasonable financial stability surprised everyone associated with the program, including myself. Also surprising and, at first puzzling, was the fact that the highly coveted reprieve which the program received from the college met with disapprobation from the PHN and the Dean of Students.

Throughout each semester the entire Student Health Service staff met each week to informally discuss clinical and administrative issues. Since the time I had submitted the budget request to the President of the college, the PHN had exempted herself from these meetings. I had requested assistance from the PHN in carrying out the negotiations with the President. This request was denied without explanation. Tension and brief verbal skirmishes erupted between us, usually over the question of my authority to undertake an independent course of action to salvage the MHP with college district funding.

Immediately after the President authorized the MHP grant, a SHS staff meeting was held, which the PHN attended. Her comments at this meeting were later reiterated in a memorandum to the President, from which I quote:

> I was not consulted regarding the increase of the (MHP) budget or its expenditures. Because of the

87

original terms of the foundation grants specifying that monies could be expended for professional salaries only, the student health service accomodated this rapid increase in professional services by providing all the supportive services and organization necessary to operate the mental health program. At the same time, the student health service increased its student intake from 837 students in Spring 1970, for a cumulative number of 996 services provided, to 2160 students seen by Spring 1972, for a cumulative number of 2873 services. Yet during this time, in spite of the increased student health services provided through coordinated efforts (e.g., dental) there was an increase of only one full-time public health nurse, one half-time secretary, a few student workers and minimal budget allocations. (PHN, 1972)

She goes on to add:

In summary, the proposed budget for the entire Student Health Service is approximately 65,000 dollars for 1972-73, while the proposed district commitment for the mental health program is 30,000 dollars, to be used with matching outside funds for the total budget of 60,000 dollars for professional salaries alone. This projects a possible mental health budget of approximately $100,000, of which 40% (excluding approbations) (sic) would continue to be absorbed in overhead by the Student Health Services.

The PHN then recommends:

(1) That CCSF contract with Westside Community Mental Health Services to provide mental health services to students on the condition that the total mental health budget provide for a completely autonomous program, e.g., all staff, supportive services, supplies, etc. This would also mean that the program could be autonomous from other student services and accountable directly to the President of the College. Assuming this Mental Health Program would be located at the Student Health Service, *all* supportive services as currently provided for by the district would have to be provided by the contracted

program or otherwise purchased from the Student Health Service.

(2) A budget providing for 1-2 mental health staff, salaried, credentialed positions under the Student Health Service.

The projection of a $100,000 Mental Health Program budget met with general incredulity, since the $60,000 allocation covered all program costs, with the exception of inexpensive supplies and two offices. The recomendations to institute an administratively autonomous Mental Health Program and to establish 1-2 "salaried-credentialed" positions in the program were categorically rejected by the President.

It is noteworthy that the two recommendations contained in the PHN's memorandum to the President were unequivocally supported by the staff of the MHP. However, the references to the burgeoning funds of the MHP as compared with the allocations for medical/nursing services, and the general tone of the memorandum, indicate that her rationales for these recommendations were not akin to those of the MHP staff.

There are several contexts for understanding the adverse reactions of the PHN to the financial growth of the MHP. The PHN was trained in and primarily loyal to the discipline of nursing. I speculate that the financial success of the MHP, when compared with the financial standstill of nursing services, probably signified to her that nursing services were of lesser status and value to the college than mental health services. Although the MHP, in terms of its college district funding (the only potential long-range source of funding), actually lacked parity with the nursing services, it had gained an economic foothold at the college which began to threaten the future dimensions of the nursing/medical programs. The PHN's dread of such a spectre was not altogether without foundation. The college administration responded to requests for additional funds for the nursing programs by pointing out that funds for the SHS were finite and metaphorically remarked that "Peter" (the MHP) had taken funds ($30,000) from "Paul" (the nursing services). The administrative tack of treating the nursing and MHP budgets as intertwined and mutually erosive, fueled the contention between the PHN and me.

A second, and perhaps more weighty factor underlying the PHN's aversion to the financial growth of the MHP is based upon the demands of the ego. "Each individual in an organization engages in two distinct types of activities, one related to the nominal purpose of the organization and the second related to the demands of his own ego" (Morowitz, 1977, p. 2).

The financial inroads of the MHP, achieved large-

90

ly without the assistance of the PHN, left her feeling
unappreciated and disfavored by the college administration. The college administration, by structuring and
defining the fiscal allocations of the nursing services
and the MHP as competitive with one another, ignored
the personal impact of such an administrative strategy.
The PHN regarded the college district subsidization of
the MHP as a personal tribute to me and a personal deprivation and humiliation to herself. The college administration's method of instituting competitive funding
for all student health services was a surefire prescrip-
tion for strife between the PHN and myself.

A second, unexpected source of resistance to the
MHP emerged when the Board of Governors ratified the
$30,000 grant. One of the Governors took the opportu-
nity to commend the services of the MHP and concluded
her comments with the suggestion that such a program
should be placed on permanent footing at the college.
Although somewhat taken aback by this dramatic windfall,
I requested, through the Dean of Students, permission
to seek a Board resolution which would provide for permanent adoption of the MHP by the college district. He
directed me to avoid the matter. In a subsequent discussion with him he indicated that permanent adoption
of the program was completely out of the question.

The Dean further explained that the Chancellor-Superintendent could make no permanent commitments to the MHP. The MHP fiscally occupied a low-priority position at the college due to the rising costs of operating the Community College District. Furthermore, the Chancellor-Superintendent philosophically favored the retention of the private, contractual system of administering the MHP. He did not regard the maintenance and delivery of mental health services as the financial responsibility of the Community College District. The Dean indicated that the Chancellor-Superintendent held strong convictions that the *raison d'etre* of the college was fundamentally to serve the educational needs of students and that mental health services were the responsibility of community agencies which were trained and legislatively mandated to provide such programs. The Dean added that the Chancellor-Superintendent enjoyed a close, compatible relationship with the highest levels of the administrative staff of the San Francisco (County) Community Mental Health Services. This relationship would be effective leverage for the eventual integration of the MHP into the county mental health system. There would be no administrative attempt to elicit the MHP staff's perspective of the pros and cons of this plan.

The Student Health Advisory Board

In the Fall of 1971, the MHP was selected by the American Psychiatric Association-National Association for Mental Health (APA-NAMH) as one of eight college mental health programs in the nation which were to be visited and studied by a team of psychology researchers. The results of this study were to appear in a publication entitled *Mental Health on the Campus*. The MHP was the only community college mental health service to be included in this study: all other programs were based at four-year colleges and universities. Each of the programs was selected for this study on the basis of "modelistic" achievements, i.e., as programs which were innovative and worthy of emulation.

The groundwork for the MHP's initial collaboration with APA-NAMH was coordinated by Mr. Leavitt. He was requested to complete a questionnaire which provided essential information about the MHP. The information which was transmitted to APA-NAMH met its requirements for the MHP's inclusion in the study. Naturally, Mr. Leavitt considered this to be a golden opportunity for the MHP to gain national recognition and prestige.

The APA-NAMH researchers arranged for a visit which would cover several days. Arrangements were made for them to meet with MHP staff and trainees, MHP clients (who volunteered to be interviewed), college administrators and members of the SHAB. There was little consultation between the SHAB and the MHP staff prior to the APA-NAMH visit. As a result, the SHAB did not recognize the possible *quid pro quo* which the MHP would derive from their cooperation with the APA-NAMH study team. In a directionless and noisy conference with the researchers, the SHAB members engaged in provocative and militant rhetoric. They expressed resentment for being "exploited" by researchers who were solely interested in "profiteering" from the sale of studies of disadvantaged students.

Prior to the APA-NAMH visit there had been a number of meetings between the SHAB and the SHS staff. With hindsight it is not difficult to recognize that these meetings were unmistakable harbingers of a later clash between the SHAB and the APA-NAMH researchers.

I believe that there were three interrelated factors which resulted in the SHAB's angry confrontation with the APA-NAMH staff. (1) Many of the SHAB members were already becoming disenchanted with inequities in the salary structure of the grant which was subsidizing their consultation work. Resentment over the higher salaries of the professional SHS staff was rapidly swelling. As indicated earlier, SHAB members were also perceiving the administrative leadership of the planning project to be "manipulative," "patronizing," and "secretive." As they themselves averred, there was a "healthy fear of being used as a rubber stamp organization." Thus, their relationship to the professional health planners was already beginning to engender feelings of economic and political exploitation.

(2) Most of the SHAB members, irrespective of their ethnic backgrounds, had experienced economic squalor and insecurity throughout their young lives. Many had also witnessed and suffered from the disorganization of their families due to economic hardship and exploitation. Thus, there was a psychological readiness to regard authority figures, particularly those in control of the allocation of funds and programs, with a great deal of suspicion. This is not to suggest that the SHAB's suspicions were excessive or unfounded in all instances. However, it does explain why the SHAB tended to be cynical about the motives of "well-intentioned" planners and researchers. I believe it also explains why they were not prepared to recognize the possible *quid pro quo* which they and the MHP would derive from their cooperation with the APA-NAMH study team.

(3) A third factor, although more geographically

remote than the others, which contributed to a sense of political exploitation, was the war in Vietnam. This faraway conflict induced feelings of exploitation among students for two important reasons. First, the war was being prosecuted by a largely White superpower against a militarily weak, Asian nation. The legitimacy of our country's role in Vietnam was unanimously invalidated by the SHAB, which strongly identified with the decided underdog in the conflict. The SHAB perceived the viciousness of the war as further evidence of the dominant society's savage disregard for and exploitation of human life.

Secondly, some of the SHAB members had already served in the Vietnam conflict and were disillusioned with their country's plunge into war. They often felt personally guilty about their participation in an "immoral" war and enraged over the fact that they allowed themselves to become entrapped and "exploited" by their government. The Vietnam veterans infused the SHAB with a strong anti-war and anti-government outlook. This outlook sometimes spread to and was confounded by the SHAB's relationships with those persons or groups which personified authority.

The male SHAB members who had not served in Vietnam (and perhaps some of the women as well) frequently felt guilty for other reasons. Some of these men had received exemptions based upon psychiatric evaluations or conscientious objection on religious grounds. In my view, some of that group felt irrational guilt because they did not endanger themselves in war, as did their veteran fellow students. Also, they felt humiliated by having to acquire sometimes dubious psychiatric or religious justifications for their exemptions, when the ugly nature of the war itself seemed reason enough to remain at home.

The confluence of the above-mentioned economic, psychological and political factors laid the groundwork for a confrontation between the SHAB and a group of White, authoritative researchers who came from Washington, D.C., the seat of the despised federal government.

The researchers were stunned by the directness and intensity of the SHAB's outpourings. They then became incensed when it was discovered that one of the SHAB members had surreptitiously tape-recorded the meeting. The director of the research team (Mr. G.) became indignant and expressed to me his unwillingness to have any further dealings with the SHAB. Although I strongly identified with the SHAB members' anger and frustration over their political exploitation, I thought their verbal onslaught short-sighted and counterproductive. In retrospect, it is clear that they had acted from a lack of knowledge regarding the wider significance and potential value of the APA-NAMH study, both to themselves and the MHP. Mr. Leavitt and I were remiss in overlooking their decided need for direction and information.

The director of the research team took most of the initiative for coordinating the meeting. He introduced the members of his team, explained the purpose of the study and directed the flow of questions and answers.

The director reacted angrily. He stated that he was interested in the SHAB's point of view, but did not wish to exchange invectives. He finally asserted that he and his staff no longer wished to tolerate the "adolescent rantings" of the SHAB and adjourned the meeting.

I strongly believe that the SHAB would have been more objective and astute had they understood the possible advantages which would have accrued to them and the MHP, from a more cooperative collaboration with the APA-NAMH researchers. For example, since the students in the SHAB were those who were most actively involved with the MHP on the campus, they could have selected a representative to attend a subsequent APA-NAMH-sponsored conference to be held in Washington, D.C. In addition, the published findings of the APA-NAMH might have provided the SHAB with positive national publicity and perhaps, in consequence, even greater political and financial support for their efforts.

The SHAB's contributions to the MHP were inestimable. In addition to its pragmatic assistance with program development, policy formulation and the hiring of staff, the SHAB provided a necessary check on any tendency on the part of the MHP to act unilaterally. Its political orientation and concerns broadened the MHP staff's interest beyond strictly clinical and administrative considerations on the campus. The staff of the MHP also felt gratified by having a unique opportunity to interact with students in a decision-making process which contrasted markedly with the more limited exchanges they were accustomed to having in conventional psychotherapeutic work with students. In general, the SHAB's regular and fiery challenges to the *status quo*, assisted the MHP in its own pursuit of institutional change and innovation.

The strength of the SHAB was in its ethnic diversity and political idealism. Although members did not always treat each other in a humanistic fashion, the SHAB, as an organization, consistently maintained a deep concern for the problems of the underprivileged and poor, and a commitment to bringing about better social conditions to help those members of society.

The weaknesses of the SHAB organization were its impatience with the glacial nature of institutional change and its tendency to discharge its indignation somewhat indiscriminately (as in the case of the APA-NAMH meeting). As a result, members were often overly disappointed with their lack of political influence to effect immediate social change. For this reason some members withdrew from the organization well before its formal demise.

In my opinion, the SHAB should be revived, providing that two conditions can be met: (1) That security and continuity be provided to the SHAB through long-range funding or credit-providing courses, and (2) that a MHP staff assignment be formally established to specifically assist the SHAB with its organizational concerns and problems, should the SHAB request such assistance.

The APA-NAMH visit was followed by a conference in Washington, D.C., to which each program would be allowed to send one staff representative and one college student. Mr. G. blacklisted all members of the SHAB from the conference and personally selected a City College student who had been a client of the MHP to participate in the Washington, D.C. proceedings.

100

Following the APA-NAMH-sponsored conference, Mr.
G. and I corresponded with each other several times in
order to exchange and augment the data which he had acquired during his visit to City College. Although he
expressed scorn and disgruntlement over the "adolescent
antics" of the SHAB, he seemed intent upon incorporating the City College MHP into the APA-NAMH publication.

Toward the end of the Spring, 1972 semester, I
received notification from Mr. G. that the MHP was being dropped from the prospective publication. I had no
forewarning of this development and considered his decision unwarranted and unfair. I immediately called Mr.
G. to ask for an explanation of his decision. He stated
that he felt he had been misled and deceived by Mr.
Leavitt, who had, in his estimation,

> enticed me into considering your program with
> some very exaggerated claims of programmatic
> accomplishments. My assessment is that your
> program is still embryonic and, although it may
> one day become fully developed, it does not mer-
> it inclusion in the publication at this time.

I challenged Mr. G.'s judgment and inquired into
the sentiments of the other members of his study team.
He admitted that they favored including the MHP, but
that his editorial discretion superceded their recommendations. I alleged that he was allowing his emotional
reactions to the SHAB to affect his objectivity. I sug-

101

gested that, although the MHP was indeed "embryonic,"
it far surpassed the accomplishments of most other community colleges and would make a unique contribution to
the publication. Moreover, no one pretended that the
MHP was on a clinical par, quantitatively at least, with
the mental health services of the affluent universities
which would be represented in the forthcoming publication. If there were programmatic deficiencies in the
MHP, they too should be mentioned. I expressed my hope
that he would realize that the national recognition
which would accrue to the MHP from being included in the
publication could be pivotal to the future survival of
the MHP. He expressed his regrets, indicated that his
decision was a *fait accompli* and offered to convey his
endorsements of the MHP to the proper City College authorities, if appropriate.

In the introduction to the publication Mr. G. re-
fers to his assessment of the MHP as follows:

> An eighth facility which was visited has not been
> included in the case studies herein. As we in-
> terviewed the various personnel connected with
> the program, it began to appear that the charac-
> teristics both of the student body and of the
> mental health service were substantially differ-
> ent from what had been our understanding from
> the information provided to us prior to our de-
> cision to include this school. More important,
> the quality of the program did not appear to be
> such that it would be appropriate to include it

among a group chosen along "modelistic" lines. We decided with particular reluctance to exclude this school, since it was our only example of a junior college and our principal example of a commuter college. (We have not, incidentally, learned in the meantime of any other junior college program that might have been included as a model.)

The disappointment which ensued from the APA-NAMH experience dampened MHP staff and SHAB morale. I decided that local publicity of the joint accomplishments of the SHAB and MHP would recoup some of that depleted morale. I discussed with the SHAB my intention to contact a local newspaper and, in detail, we planned how best to publicize our efforts. The result was the highly positive *San Francisco Chronicle* article which was quoted earlier. The SHAB members were inspired by the widespread recognition they received from the publicity. This served to cement the relationship between the SHAB and the MHP, which had been temporarily estranged due to the APA-NAMH debacle.

The eventual demise of the SHAB, in the summer of 1972, was entirely predictable. The planning grant which had subsidized the salaries of the SHAB members expired at that time. Although there were modest attempts by the SHS staff to revive the SHAB in the Fall of 1972, the lack of financial incentive for participation was crucial. Although the alternative of offering academic credit for SHAB participation was explored, students were understandably reluctant to make time-consuming and sometimes expensive (members with children often had to pay child-care costs during the time they were serving on the SHAB) commitments to the SHAB without financial remuneration. Since the college administration did not support the concept of the SHAB, funds for its continuance could not be procured from the Community College District. The expiration of funding was a deathblow to the vibrant and principled student organization.

The Ascendancy of a Psychological Trainee to the Position of Clinical Coordinator

In the Spring of 1972, I appointed a successor, Ms. Myrna Quan Holden, to the administrative position which I had formerly held: MHP Clinical Coordinator (CC). There were no formalized procedures for implementing this appointment, and I took advantage of the administrative latitude this afforded me by independently appointing a woman who had served in the MHP as a psychological trainee for over a year. Although she was relatively inexperienced, clinically and administratively, she demonstrated excellent potential for professional leadership in the MHP.

The appointment was problematic because there were two candidates who were qualified and eligible for the CC position. Ms. Quan Holden (who is now the Co-Director of the MHP) views the experience of her being appointed in the following way:

> I was not aware of the process which resulted in my being hired. I did assume it was your (my) decision. I naturally was tickled, but insecure. Because there was no formalized process, I didn't feel I was bona fide, not really sure of how seriously I would be taken. This was complicated by the fact that two other trainees (both of whom were Black, and one of whom was the sole competitor for the CC position) told me I was selected because I was a passive Chinese female, who could be easily controlled.

Admittedly, the unilateral hiring of Ms. Quan Holden was clearly antithetical to the humanistic ideals to which I aspire. I consider that administrative action to be the most authoritarian decision I have made throughout my tenure as director of the MHP. As I will explain, the unilateral method used to hire Ms. Quan Holden tended to obscure her professional responsibilities and impair, to a degree, her relationships with other MHP staff.

Additional complications arose.

> There was no job description. My authority and responsibilities were vague. Because you were so casual and didn't spell out my responsibilities, I felt unclear about the appointment. I felt like a floater, being asked to do something, but not sure what it was. My insecurities were aggravated by the fact that we had a staff psychiatrist then who earned a higher salary than I did and who was often consulted by you on administrative matters. I really didn't know if and when I should be included in those consultations. (Ms. Quan Holden)

The role of professional inexperience was also a factor.

> I was inexperienced and insecure, as well as
> lacking in political understanding. This made
> it difficult for me to be assertive. You and I
> didn't know each other well then, which made it
> difficult to know how much we should collabor-
> ate. I was not aware of the administrative work
> which you were doing in order to maintain the
> MHP. I guess, with implicit confidence in you,
> I just assumed you were taking care of things
> and that it would all work out well in the end.
> You might say I was ignorantly blissful. (Ms.
> Quan Holden)

A perceptible shift begins to take place in Ms.

Quan Holden's administrative *modus operandi* after about

one year.

> I felt freer after the staff psychiatrist left.
> Although he was clinically supportive, his af-
> fect upon me was stifling. I had a tendency
> to defer to the authority of his position and
> discipline (Ms. Quan Holden is a counseling psy-
> chologist). I began to assume more administra-
> tive responsibilities, beginning with the super-
> vision of graduate students. (Ms. Quan Holden)

The transition from the status of psychological

trainee to Clinical Coordinator was an administrative

leap of considerable proportion. Such factors as the

extent of professional experience and personal securi-

ty certainly help to determine the pace and quality of

one's adaptation to such a change of roles. Neverthe-

less, many of the ambiguities and uncertainties which

Ms. Quan Holden encountered were inevitable by-products

of the fluid, and as yet underdeveloped, administrative

structure of the MHP.

Firstly, since there had been no formalized procedure for the hiring of the original MHP staff, there was no serviceable precedent for hiring Ms. Quan Holden. When one is hired as the personal choice of another, without the imprimatur of bureaucratic policies and procedures to legitimate the process officially, self-doubts naturally arise over how truly qualified one is for a position in the organization.

Secondly, since no definitive job descriptions were delineated for the clinical and administrative positions in the MHP, professional roles and responsibilities were vague and perhaps duplicative. When I had been Clinical Coordinator, I commonly could not discern where my job administratively ended and Mr. Leavitt's began. When I assumed the directorship of the MHP, I retained many of my former administrative tasks, while assuming the completely new and extensive responsibilities of the directorship. Doing so, of course, left Ms. Quan Holden in an administrative limbo. The lack of clearly established job functions and responsibilities resulted in the assumption of administrative tasks based largely upon expediency and professional expertise and adeptness, rather than official organizational requirements.

The negative consequences of nebulous organizational rules and requirements were confusion and tentativeness in relation to respective job responsibilities. On the other hand, the lack of rigid and deeply ingrained job requirements allowed Ms. Quan Holden and me to refine our perspectives of our assignments and to discover gradually how we would most effectively complement and supplement each other's work. In that respect, the bureaucratic underdevelopment of the MHP was a decided advantage to its administrative personnel.

> Since job descriptions are really part of a bureau's rules, they also cannot be designed in advance to fit every situation that actually occurs. In any organization with formal job descriptions, the particular abilities and personality of the individual assigned to each job will never mesh perfectly with the tasks he is supposed to carry out. As a result, several types of adaptation occur.
>
> First, tasks formally assigned to one person are in fact performed by one or more others. These others may have superior capabilities, their personalities may be better suited to the tasks, they may be more willing to do the work, or they just cannot escape it as easily. Second, some formally assigned tasks may not be done at all, or may be done poorly. Third, some activities carried out in pursuit of the bureau's formal goals will not yet be part of the formal assignment structure. For example, every time an official is developing something new, he will necessarily be acting outside of the existing formal structure of assigned tasks. (Downs, 1967, pp. 63-64)

These three types of adaptation exemplified the informal structure of the MHP at the time of the appointment of Ms. Quan Holden. First, although I assigned a

set of official tasks to Ms. Quan Holden, I actually
assumed the lion's share of those very tasks myself.
Second, since Ms. Quan Holden was "not sure what it
was" that was being formally assigned, she regarded me
as the program bulwark and undertook few administrative
tasks herself. Third, the lack of a "formal assignment
structure" allowed me to interact closely with the SHAB
and to lobby the faculty in quest of college funding;
activities which were essential in pursuing the organization's formal goals, but which were "outside of the
existing formal structure of assigned tasks" at that
time.

The Pursuit of Manpower Assistance and Funding From the Community Mental Health Services

Although I did not agree with the Chancellor/Su-
perintendent's plan to integrate the MHP into the county
mental health system, I did support the principle of a
close relationship between that organization and the MHP.
The WCMHS, which already was the lone source of funding
among the county's agencies, gave partisan endorsement
to enlisting other county agencies in providing financial and manpower assistance to the MHP. The first county agency which was besought for such purposes was the
Mission Mental Health Service. An application for as-

sistance to this agency was abortive, as indicated in the earlier discussion of the SHAB's role in the development of programs within the MHP. An application to this agency for assistance was unsuccessful, after the SHAB and the MHP discovered that the Mission Mental Health Center Director intended to have his staff provide psychological services only to those students who were Mission district residents. That administrative requirement was rejected as elitist and parochial. No further negotiations took place between the MHP and the Mission Mental Health Center following this episode.

I then requested a conference with the Executive Director of the Northeast Mental Health Service (NEMHS). This conference was attended and led by an administrative assistant. I was asked to describe the MHP and to offer justification for an allocation of funds and/or manpower from the NEMHS. I stressed the fact that about 15% of the students who were receiving services in the MHP were Northeast residents. Not only was the MHP absorbing some of the potential caseload of NEMHS, thereby reducing NEMHS program costs, but the early treatment which many students received in the MHP averted serious psychiatric crises which could become a considerable drain upon the community agency, should those students turn to NEMHS for assistance. I added that the placement of community agency personnel in the MHP would strengthen our programmatic ties and foster our common goals.

When I concluded my comments, the administrative assistant stated that he wished to ask me what might be construed as an embarrassing question, but one which he felt obliged to raise with all applicants for agency assistance. He asked if I were really seeking his agency's assistance not because the MHP was a vital service, but because I was desperately trying to protect or save my job. In other words, weren't my concerns primarily self-serving?

After a moment's reflection, I told him that the question was not an embarrassing one to me. Rather, I thought it a stupid question and one which he might find embarrassing to himself for its stupidity. I pointed out that if my concerns were largely self-oriented, I probably would not foolishly admit that to him. However, since I had strong professional convictions about the MHP's value to City College students (which I had already reported to him at great length), I considered his impugnation of my integrity quite ugly and stupid. Our dialogue ended in an exchange of piercing glares.

In my view, the administrative assistant and I

clashed because we had diametrically opposing professional interests and objectives. My concerns were
clearly to gain financial and/or manpower assistance
from the NEMHS. I realized from previous experiences
with the county agencies that my chances for success
were slim. Therefore, I attempted to be very forceful
and persuasive in presenting the rationales for my application for assistance. In my opinion, the Executive
Director of the NEMHS had already decided, for whatever
reason, that the MHP was not to be a recipient of his
agency's assistance. Rather than deal with me directly and in objective terms, he delegated the unpleasant
task of rebuffing my proposal to his assistant, who
countered the appeals of community groups with personal
deprecations.

My own strong reaction to the administrative assistant was, I think, based upon two factors: (1) I
immediately resented the fact that the Executive Director used his administrative assistant as a buffer between us; (2) I was obviously submitting an appeal not
only in behalf of the MHP, but also, as the administrative assistant charged, to serve my own interests. I
never believed that my concerns for the MHP were purely
altruistic, nor did I believe that my self-interests
(to retain my employment in the MHP) were detrimental to

the MHP. However, I perceived that the administrative assistant was attempting to bastardize my concerns for the MHP by suggesting that they were largely self-serving and, by implication, possibly incompatible with the interests of the MHP. The off-hand manner in which I thought this implication was put to me by a person who had known nothing about me or my commitment to the MHP before our meeting was insulting and infuriating. My sharp words were obviously not intended to change his sentiments about me or my proposal; however, I had, by that time, already reached the sorry conclusion that the NEMHS would not lend assistance to the MHP. Thus, I forsook diplomacy in favor of salvaging my self-esteem.

I was advised by the Executive Director, who said very little during the meeting, to call him in about a month. He advised me to speak with a particular member of the NEMHS Board of Directors in the meantime about my application. He indicated that he would refer the matter to this board member who, in turn, would request a final ruling on the application from the Board of Directors. A week later I called the board member to whom I was referred. She indicated that she had heard nothing about the application from the Executive Director.

113

Over the next two months I placed many telephone calls to the designated board member. She each time repeated that the Executive Director was keeping her in ignorance of my application. I also called the Executive Director many times, but he was always unavailable for my calls. I left instructions for him to return my calls, but none were ever returned. The pursuit of assistance from the NEMHS became a palpably hopeless venture and eventually was unceremoniously dropped.

The next application for county assistance was directed to the Sunset Mental Health Services. This agency appeared to be the likeliest organizational candidate to support the MHP since the largest plurality of students who received MHP services (usually 25-35%) were residents of the Sunset district. Ms. Quan Holden and I were invited to make a presentation to the Sunset Board of Directors. Although the responses of that board were generally favorable and sympathetic to the MHP, its ultimate resolution was to reject our application for assistance. The rejection was allegedly based upon agency priorities at that time, which were primarily geared to establishing psychotherapeutic programs for young children and the aged.

The Dean of Students, at the behest of the Chancellor-Superintendent, frequently reminded me of the

114

essentiality of gaining county subvention and sponsorship for the MHP. I had kept him abreast of the mis-
haps and impediments which had been encountered in our
dealings with the various county mental health centers.
He assured me that the Chancellor-Superintendent had
important sway with the highest administrative echelons
of the San Francisco County Mental Health Services and
that this influence would yield financial and programmatic benefits to the MHP. I indicated to the Dean that
I would continue to cooperate with the plan to win county
support for the MHP, despite deep personal misgivings.
My reservations were based upon an expectation that an
administrative integration with the county mental health
system would portend the eventual ouster of present MHP
personnel, including Ms. Quan Holden and me.

This prognostication was based upon two ominous
factors: (1) Should the county assume administrative
control of the MHP, it would be able to exercise wide
discretion in hiring the personnel to work in the MHP.
If the current personnel of the MHP were forced to compete with county employees for positions in the MHP, it
was likely that the county, serving as the organizational employer, would give preferential consideration to
its own staff. The county was reputed, by many mental
health practitioners, within and without its system, to

be an organization which was rife with nepotism and mutual "back-scratching." Despite their proven qualifications for jobs which they already held, the MHP staff foresaw that they would lose their positions, as a result of a "rigged" county administered hiring procedure, to their county counterparts.

(2) All the mental health positions in the county were under the jurisdiction of the Civil Service. Consequently, in the event that the MHP became integrated into the county system, those who already held Civil Service positions with the county could preempt those who did not enjoy Civil Service status. Since MHP staff did not enjoy Civil Service status, they would have to await the development of openings in the Civil Service system and then, through a series of professional examinations, prove qualified for positions which they already held in the MHP. To compete within a system which was purportedly fraught with patronage and which imposed stringent Civil Service requirements was a risk which the MHP staff were loathe to take.

Thus, it was necessary to seek county assistance, without allowing the Chancellor-Superintendent to effect his plan for full county adoption of the MHP. I will return to this subject in the next chapter in order to describe how such a delicate balance was

116

struck.

The Altered and Problematic Relationship Between the Mental Health Program and Its Sponsoring Agencies

In order to study the altered and problematic relationship between the MHP and its sponsoring agencies I will concentrate upon two distinguishing characteristics of those organizations: (1) their unique styles of communication; and (2) their organizational priorities.

The WCMHS is an agency which is largely staffed and administered by Black professionals. The majority of its Board of Directors is also Black. The style of communication of both staff and lay community leaders tends to be direct, often strident and pregnant with Black ghetto vernacular and humor. Although the language and style of communication can be intimidating to the uninitiated, the relative lack of dissimulation and empty diplomacy provide a clarity to issues under inter-agency negotiation. If one finds it possible to re-spect rather than resent the angry tirades which some-times erupt from community leaders, there is ample op-portunity to determine exactly what is being demanded and how those demands can be met.

In terms of programmatic priorities for its mem-ber agencies, the WCMHS was not indifferent to the de-

livery of high-quality care for psychiatric patients.
However, the priority which always came to the fore in
my work with the WCMHS was the need for hiring ethnic
minority personnel in satisfactory percentages. If a
determination were made that an agency was derelict in
its commitment to the principle of ethnic minority representation, that agency could not redeem itself with
the WCMHS, regardless of its countervailing achievements
and qualities.

The following examples illustrate both the predominant style of communication and the organizational
priorities of the WCMHS.

Soon after I had assumed the directorship of the
MHP, I was invited to attend a meeting of the Board of
Directors of the WCMHS in order to report on the MHP
and to answer the board's questions. I had mistakenly
presupposed that the WCMHS was already conversant with
the staff and clinical workings of the MHP; therefore,
I came to the meeting somewhat unprepared for what was
to transpire.

After a short, uneventful presentation, the
board members asked questions. The initial questioning
went smoothly and satisfactorily. I then met with
criticism regarding the academic nursing department of
City College. That program had been assailed by the

WCMHS for allegedly maintaining a racist admissions and hiring policy, and a few board members inadvertently confused it with the MHP. The confusion was resolved by a clarifying statement from one of the board members:

> A motion was adopted to direct a communication to the Office of Federal Contract Compliance and to the Compliance Officer of HEW objecting to the affirmative action program which has been filed with them from City College and ask them to hold up any further federal funding to City College until they can come up with a meaningful affirmative action policy in the City College nursing program. (Minutes, Board Meeting, Jan. 6, 1972)

I then was doggedly questioned by an outspoken member of the board who asked for an ethnic breakdown of the "psychiatric" staff of the MHP. I misunderstood the question, as I later discovered, to mean the ethnic composition of the staff of psychiatrists in the MHP at that time. Although more than 50% of the entire MHP staff were from ethnic minorities, two of the three part-time consulting psychiatrists were White; the other was Latino. In a moment of panic I responded by answering that the three psychiatrists were White. The board member interpreted my answer to mean that the entire "psychiatric" staff of the MHP was White. With a virulence which frightened me, he denounced the MHP as racist and called for a review of its funding status.

119

> As per the Board's request the MHP administra-
> tive director presented a verbal report in ad-
> dition to a written report which had been mailed
> to the Board in advance. He gave a general
> description of the kinds of activities in which
> the project involves itself. Due to inquiry as
> to the ethnic breakdown of the staff employed
> in the project the Board resolved that more
> minority group people should be hired.
> (Minutes, Board Meeting, Jan. 6, 1972)

The bland wording of the minutes of the board meeting belies the emotional intensity of the criticisms and threats which were hurled at the MHP and me. I made an attempt to rebut the allegations, but the Chairperson of the meeting called for closure of the discussion. As I was leaving the meeting, a White psychiatrist quipped to me, "Welcome to the real world." My angry reply was, "Fuck that, I grew up in the real world. I'll work this thing out yet."

The next day I called the Executive Director of the WCMHS, who informed me that I had made a poor report to the board and that he had not realized that the MHP was so deficient in meeting the requirements and standards of the WCMHS with respect to attaining an ethnically balanced staff. I took the opportunity to correct his impressions by enumerating the ethnic background of each staff member of the MHP. He indicated that, in his opinion, the program had an adequate ethnic mix and that I should seek to correct the faulty impressions which I left with the board the previous evening.

I immediately requested permission to speak with the WCMHS Personnel Committee, the Chairperson of which was the board member who had charged the MHP with racist practices. When I attempted to review for the Personnel Committee the hiring practices and policies of the MHP, the Chairperson foreclosed all discussion of the matter on the grounds that the MHP was in violation of Fair Employment Practices legislation. The Executive Director then interceded by asking the Chairperson to reconsider since new information about the MHP staff's ethnic composition had surfaced since the board meeting.

The Chairperson relented and after auditing each position in the MHP strictly on an ethnic basis, he apologized for his earlier comments. The issue of the MHP's commitment to the hiring of minority personnel was never raised again throughout the tenure of the relationship between the MHP and the WCMHS.

A few months later, the WCMHS instituted a computerized "tracking" system which required that each member agency submit vital data regarding their patients to a central data bank. The data were utilized to apprise each agency of the prior services which had been rendered to the patient by other agencies within the consortium. This system would enable participating agencies to better complement each other's programmatic efforts in behalf of the patient and would tend to preclude duplication of therapeutic services.

The WCMHS was convinced that the confidentiality of the data collection system was ironclad and gave such assurances to the MHP staff. Certain of the MHP staff, however, particularly the politically radical members and the Coordinator of SHS (a public health nurse who had replaced the original PHN-Coordinator), raised objections to the requirements imposed by the WCMHS. Their objections were largely based upon a disbelief that the confidentiality of students would be protected.

The research team of the WCMHS visited the college in order to explain and justify the newly instituted system. Evidently, it had not met with opposition elsewhere in the WCMHS consortium, and there was puzzlement and impatience with the lack of cooperation and delays which took place in instituting the system of data collection at City College.

At this meeting the Coordinator of the SHS and several of the MHP staff challenged the foolproofness of the data collection system. The researchers were criticized for invading the privacy of City College students.

Although I had qualms about the efficacy and confidentiality of the system, I was inclined to adopt the plan
without further argument. However, I also did not wish
to dismiss the protestations of the MHP staff by quickly
acquiescing to the researchers' demands. Therefore, I
temporized by requesting that the MHP be temporarily exempted from the data collection system until an alternative method of acquiring and transmitting data could
be devised. The researchers, who had spent many months
carefully planning and promulgating their project, were
affronted by the resistance of the MHP staff to its immediate adoption.

A second meeting was called at the WCMHS office.
At this meeting the WCMHS Director of Research refused
to consider any proposals to deviate from the data collection system of his agency. He stated in unequivocal
terms that the system was designed to work effectively
and that if he and his staff could not be trusted to implement their plans in a professionally ethical and competent manner, there was little purpose in discussing
the matter further. The intransigence of the MHP staff
and the WCMHS researchers left them at loggerheads until
one of the WCMHS administrators (who was later to become
its Executive Director) intervened.

I stated that the White hippies in the MHP

123

couldn't understand how poor Black people in the Westside District were going to be enormously helped by the data collection system. They (the hippies) were too busy giving lip service to their phony ideals.

I rebutted this statement by mentioning that the strongest objections to the researchers' proposal came from Third World staff members of the MHP. He went on to say: "Adopt the data collection system or forfeit WCMHS funding. Take it or leave it, but let's cut out all this bullshit."

The MHP staff opted to adopt the data collection system. Incidentally, the worst fears of the MHP staff regarding the question of confidentiality did not mateerialize.

The CMCP was staffed and administered entirely by White clinicians. Most of the psychotherapists and administrators had been trained in psychoanalytically-oriented psychotherapy. The predominant style of communication tended to be characterized by tact, intellectualisms and psychological jargon. Humor was very evident, but stridency and emotionalism were anathematic. As a result, intra-staff expectations and feelings were often ambiguous and the course of action necessary for the resolution of administrative problems was also apt to be ambiguous. In order to accurately decipher administrative requests and intentions it was often necessary to resort to psychological inference and intuition.

In terms of programmatic priorities, the CMCP was strongly committed to the delivery of high-quality psychotherapeutic services to its patients. However, the foremost priority which emerged in dealing administratively with the CMCP in 1972 was the financial and personal status of its Medical Director. Thus, personnel within the agency who disregarded or flouted his administrative authority and importance, regardless of their clinical or administrative expertise, were held in contempt and, as will be illustrated, were sometimes terminated from employment.

The following example illustrates the predominant style of communication and the programmatic priorities of the CMCP. Upon returning from his sabbatical, Mr. Leavitt expected to resume his erstwhile role as Administrative Director of the CMCP. He learned, however, that the person who had served as his interim replacement was to remain as an agency administrator and that they would serve together as Co-Directors of the CMCP. This administrative revamping was primarily instigated by the Medical Director, who received full support for the change from the CMCP Board of Directors. The altered administrative structure of the CMCP quickly proved untenable as administrative duties overlapped and conflicted.

The Board of Directors and the Medical Director next resolved to restructure Mr. Leavitt's assignment by requiring that he devote his clinical time to community projects. He was to generate new psychotherapeutic programs which would be sponsored and financed by local corporations and unions. This was clearly a Sisyphean task, since the national and local economies were undergoing a recession at the time.

At the time of these events, I had a dual relationship with the CMCP. As Administrative Director of the MHP, I was accountable to both Co-Directors of the CMCP, although administrative consultations were exclusively with Mr. Leavitt. I also "moonlighted" at the CMCP as a staff psychotherapist. When Mr. Leavitt began to suffer administrative setbacks at the CMCP, a faction of the staff, of which I was member, protested the administrative measures which were being taken by the Medical Director and the Board of Directors.

The staff of the CMCP were initially given assurances that Mr. Leavitt would be provided a satisfactory administrative niche in the agency. The Medical Director stated that there was no intention to endanger Mr. Leavitt's status or stature in the clinic.

126

We were told that decisions to modify his assignment were undertaken solely on pragmatic grounds, i.e., in consideration of budgetary factors. The dissident staff's perception of the conflict was that the Medical Director had taken advantage of Mr. Leavitt's sabbatical leave of absence to carry out a grudge (for the previous professional restraints which Mr. Leavitt had placed upon him) by undercutting and eventually eliminating his position at the clinic. This was emphatically denied by the Medical Director.

In the Spring of 1973, Mr. Leavitt received a formal notice of termination from the CMCP Board of Directors. In protest, a segment of the clinical staff, myself included, defected from the clinic in order to reorganize as a group practice. This mass exodus of clinical staff seriously destabilized the CMCP, at least temporarily, since most of their patients, on their own volition, went with the departing staff, thereby producing a financial crisis for the clinic. My own voluntary resignation from the CMCP as a staff psychotherapist was a calculated risk, since I technically was still employed by the clinic by virtue of my directorship of the MHP, which continued to be sponsored by the CMCP.

Certainly, the CMCP would re-evaluate and perhaps

consider severing its affiliation with the MHP now that
I had already left the clinic as a disgruntled staff
psychotherapist. The first step in the re-evaluation
process was a request from the Medical Director to confer with him. In that conference there were requests
for factual information about the clinical services of
the MHP; however, this tack appeared to me to be a pre-
text for raising two interrelated issues which were of
primary interest to the Medical Director: (1) whether
he could begin to take a more active and central role
in the MHP; and (2) whether, in doing so, he could be
financially remunerated for his time and services.

Both issues were taken under consideration; however, the final arbiter would be the WCMHS, which determined the appropriateness of all budgetary requests. The WCMHS determined that the CMCP Medical
Director was not entitled to financial remuneration
for his services.

> The $3,600 figure earmarked for the Medical
> Director was not included in the budget due to
> Westside's view that such administrative costs
> should be absorbed by each agency for all on-
> going programs. We will no doubt be discussing
> this issue further at our future meetings.
> (Amada, Spring 1973)

The Medical Director had nominally served with
the MHP for three years (by dint of his medical directorship of the CMCP) without a fee; therefore, there

seemed to be no sound reason for a newly established salary for his services. Also, the WCMHS could not determine a clinical or administrative justification for increasing his time or enlarging his professional role in the MHP.

The WCMHS's firm blockage of the Medical Director's aspirations *vis a vis* the MHP was a strong propellant of further conflict and estrangement between the MHP and CMCP. The penultimate step in deciding to disengage administratively from the CMCP came in the following letter from the Medical Director.

> The Executive Committee met to discuss the issue of the City College project. After full discussion it was decided to recommend to the Board of Directors that the Clinic end its affiliation with this project and not renew a contract for the 1973-74 period.

I was then requested to attend a Board of Directors meeting in order to discuss the future sponsorship of the MHP. At this meeting the board expressed reservations about continuing its sponsorship of the MHP on the grounds that the CMCP was deriving no tangible benefits from its association with the college program. Furthermore, when an attempt was made to develop closer ties between the CMCP and the MHP by augmenting the Medical Director's role in the MHP, the WCMHS suppressed the effort. I was asked to conjec-

ture on what I would do if the CMCP dissolved its administrative sponsorship of the MHP and if I was desirous of a dissolution of our relationship.

I responded to the board's questions by commenting that I was not desirous of a severance of
our relationship, mentioning jokingly that my first
response to such a decision would be to perspire a
great deal and adding seriously that termination of
the CMCP sponsorship would require that the MHP seek
organizational asylum elsewhere, although the staff
of the MHP were not eager to embark on such a course
of action.

Soon after this meeting, I sent the following
letter to the CMCP Medical Director:

> I must share my concern over a matter of irri-
> tation to me. I had the clear impression from
> my meeting with you (the Medical Director and
> the Board) that you expected I might contest
> the CMCP decision to terminate. Frankly, I
> have never even been tempted to do so. Obvi-
> ously, the relationship between CMCP and the
> City College program becomes totally untenable
> when the host agency (as represented by the
> Executive Committee) recommends termination and
> any consideration of altering that fact would
> be naive.

Notification of the final termination of the
CMCP sponsorship of the MHP came in the following letter from the Medical Director:

> This letter is to serve as 60 days notice of

130

cancellation of the Westside contract covering the City College Project. In consideration of your request, we are amenable to an interim sponsorship ending August 31, 1973; however, our hope is that you will find an appropriate host agency prior to that date. We extend our best wishes for the continued success of this very worthwhile project.

Styles of Communication

As suggested earlier, the differential styles of communication of the WCMHS and the CMCP placed enormous demands upon the administrators of the MHP to effectively interpret and resolve the expectations of those agencies. The very survival of the MHP depended upon an accurate reading of their administrative intentions and expectations.

In the case of the WCMHS, the style of communication was blunt, at times strident and malaproprian, and unambiguous. The absence of mainstream language was, on balance, an advantage, not a handicap, to the negotiations between the WCMHS and the MHP. The language of the outspoken lay and professional leaders of the WCMHS expressed trenchantly what was considered amiss and what had to be carried out in the MHP in order to rectify administrative deficiencies. The intent and choices were not beclouded by euphemisms. The style of communication of the WCMHS community optimized its potential for achieving

131

programmatic objectives.

It is a tenet of linguistics -- although perhaps more an article of faith than the result of experimental demonstration -- that any language or variety is adequate for any demand which the speech community can make upon it. Ultimately, then, all speakers would be equal in the number and complexity of "ideas" or "messages" which their language enables them to communicate -- although we know perfectly well that the ideas and messages are themselves sometimes different. Most of the favorite examples of the "poverty" of ghetto language are subject to the same strictures that linguists have always had against other attempts of the same type. (Dillard, 1972, p. 257)

Dillard adds:

In spite of having accepted, formally, the standards of correctness of the advantaged white community, the Black community retains an impressive amount of cultural and linguistic solidarity. (Dillard, 1972, p. 262)

The WCMHS expressed and maintained its cultural and organizational solidarity, to a considerable extent, through Black dialect. Although this dialect might be alien and unnerving to one accustomed to genteel modes of communication, the blunt and direct linguistic style of the WCMHS spokesmen aided the administrators of the MHP in determining exactly why a charge of racism had been leveled at the MHP and how such a charge could be redressed. Thus, my confidence that "I'll work this thing out yet."

When the MHP staff balked at adopting the WCMHS data collection system, the "take it (the data collection system) or leave it (the WCMHS funding), but no more bullshit" retort made the intent of WCMHS painfully clear. The bluntness and vulgarism facilitated administrative decision-making in the MHP.

The CMCP was a very different linguistic "cup of tea." Although emotions ran high in that agency when Mr. Leavitt's position was first undermined and later eliminated, the style of communication tended to be low-key and euphemistic. Mr. Leavitt was not demoted; rather "reassigned." He was not being removed from the daily activities of the clinic; rather he was being given a "challenging opportunity to generate new community programs." The CMCP's intellectualized style of communication camouflaged the true nature of the intense conflicts within the embattled agency. Thus, many of the CMCP staff, perhaps including Mr. Leavitt, assumed a gradualist approach to dealing with administrative changes which they regarded as highly objectionable. The euphemistic style of communicating traumatic administrative decisions engendered false hopes in a staff which preferred to believe that the firing of a long-time and deeply admired colleague "could not happen here." Thus, they were professionally impotent to overturn a series of admininstrative decisions to which they strenuously objected.

The style of communication which is characterized by excessive tact, psychological jargon and euphemistic terminology has been termed by one writer "official language." Perhaps official language is the
first refuge of an uncourageous administration: "Official language often reveals a lack of courage"
(Brook, 1973, p. 89). Brook goes on to suggest that
the user of official language is afraid to make a
plain statement that could be challenged or that
could commit others to action. The Board of Directors and the Medical Director of the CMCP discouraged
staff challenges and commitments to action by making
piecemeal decisions which led to the eventual ouster
of Mr. Leavitt and the MHP, always carefully eschewing
plain statements (until final decisions were reached)
that that was their intent.

Another writer suggests that as a general rule,
"Whenever the social function of a learned vocabulary
becomes more important to the users than its communicative function, communication suffers and jargon
proliferates" (Hayakawa, 1964, p. 287). The social
function of the "learned vocabulary" of the CMCP
Board of Directors and the Medical Director was to
thwart and defang staff opposition to Mr. Leavitt's

administrative demotions and eventual termination. Through the use of soothing banalities such as "administrative reassignment," "generating new programs" and "budgetary considerations," the communicative function (to notify the staff that Mr. Leavitt was being gradually removed from the CMCP) was attenuated. In deciding the fate of the MHP, I was asked to "conjecture upon a future without CMCP sponsorship. The social function of such a "tactful" query was to preclude, in my opinion, hostile, emotional objections to that prospect.

If we can accept one definition of politics as the "activity concerned with achieving control, advancement, or some other goal in a nongovernmental group" (Webster's Dictionary, 1970), the CMCP, by firing Mr. Leavitt and terminating the MHP, was carrying out dramatic political measures. Orwell (1945, p. 261) suggests that political language is essential to the efficient implementation of repugnant political activity: "Political language has to consist of euphemism, question-begging and sheer cloudy vagueness."

The use of official or political language had the effect of delaying and defusing political action within the CMCP. This factor strongly contributed to the inability of the CMCP staff to counteract the gradual demotions and ultimate firing of Mr. Leavitt. It also contributed to unnecessary delays and pressures in resolving the matter of future organizational sponsorship of the MHP.

I wish to point out that I am not imputing a superiority to any particular style of communication. Within the context of my administrative work with the MHP's sponsoring agencies I personally favored the general linguistic style of the WCMHS to the mainstream style of communication which prevailed at the CMCP. My preference was largely based upon two factors: (1) My administrative dealings with each agency were rather sporadic and brief. Consequently, in the interests of time, it was imperative to receive direct and clearly formulated administrative communications, even if orders were sometimes couched in intimidating terms. The bluntness of the linguistic style of the WCMHS readily lent itself to administrative action. The communication style of the CMCP was personally less jarring; however, due to its sometimes ambiguous and dissimulative quality, administrative decisions had to be delayed until there was greater clarity. Such delays, particularly during the formative years of the MHP, could be quite detrimental to the program.

(2) A second reason underlying my preference for the linguistic style of the WCMHS is strictly personal. I grew up in a neighborhood of Newark, New Jersey which was quite similar racially and economically to the Westside district of San Francisco. For a substantial period of that time I strongly identified with and shared the vernacular and linguistic style of the Black community with which I closely interacted. That linguistic style has remained an ineradicable part of me, and I occasionally rely upon it, particularly when I am angry. For that reason, when the MHP experienced conflicts with both the CMCP and the WCMHS, I felt more "at home" in dealing with the style of communication which was prevalent within the latter agency. Admittedly, in more relaxed social or professional circumstances I prefer to indulge in a mainstream linguistic style. However, such a style of communication was not conducive to implementing administrative decisions quickly, and delays during the early years of the MHP could be quite harmful to the status of the program.

The Search for Mental Health Program Sponsorship

In the ensuing months I conducted a frenetic search for MHP sponsorship from social service and psychiatric agencies in San Francisco. An application for agency sponsorship which was submitted to Children's Hospital of San Francisco was quickly rejected on the grounds that the MHP seemed too peripheral to the interests and priorities of that organization.

> Assuming administrative sponsorship of the MHP was a matter of increasing our clinical responsibilities with very little to gain thereby. At the time of your application, Children's Hospital was going through a painful reorganization and the hospital administration was not supportive of psychiatry. Questions arose as to who would be medically and administratively responsible for a college program operated somewhere else -- this made everyone wary of the venture. I'd say it boiled down to who would be able to control and vouch for the services of the MHP, administratively and medically.
> (Director of Adult Psychiatry, Children's
> Hospital)

I then sought and received an invitation to submit an application in person to the San Francisco Suicide Prevention Board of Directors. I was assisted by the Executive Director of WCMHS. The outcome of of the board meeting is described as follows:

> We had to reject your proposal for Suicide Prevention sponsorship of the MHP for two reasons: (1) the insurance coverage for Suicide Prevention could not be extended to a psychotherapeutic program such as the MHP, and (2) the staff of Suicide Prevention had no strong personal or programmatic ties to the MHP; therefore, nobody was up for it (sponsoring the MHP).
> (Chairperson, Program Committee, Suicide
> Prevention)

138

Because a new agency sponsor was not secured
by August 31, the CMCP reluctantly agreed to extend
their sponsorship of the MHP into the Fall semester
of 1973. The MHP was able eventually to negotiate
a contract with Progress Foundation of San Francisco.
The means by which this contract was consummated will
be discussed in the next chapter.

The Origins of Rapport Between the Mental Health Program and the City College Board of Governors

In the Spring semester, 1972, I was requested
to present a report on the activities of the MHP to
the City College Board of Governors. The report received lukewarm responses from the board until I
mentioned the fact that the MHP was to be included
in a national publication which described "modelistic" college mental health services (it had not
yet been excluded from the APA-NAMH publication).

> You kiddingly stated that you didn't know
> why the APA-NAMH would select the MHP as a
> model program. The board member, Mr. S.,
> a White attorney, perked up and said the pro-
> gram was selected because it must have de-
> served the recognition. The enthusiasm ex-
> uded by Mr. S. aroused our interest in this
> board member as a possible future ally.
> (Ms. Quan Holden)

During the Spring semester I attended the
classes of many instructors in order to make presentations in behalf of the MHP. As a result, a number

139

of positive relationships developed, one of which was
with the sister of the Board member, Mr. S. She reported to me that Mr. S. had a very favorable view of
the MHP, indicating that he would probably be very
receptive to assisting the MHP, should the need
arise.

Later in the Spring, the budget request of
$30,000 was placed before the Board of Governors
for ratification.

> Mr. S. made several friendly comments about
> the MHP, but then Ms. X, a Black educator,
> unexpectedly extolled the program as one
> which was essential to the needs of minority
> students in particular. She then opined that
> such a program should be considered for per-
> manent adoption by the college, since its
> value was unassailable. For a brief moment
> I thought there would be board action to ad-
> dress the question of program permanency;
> however, the discussion quickly dissipated and
> then was dropped. I had the sense that it
> was squelched, but I don't know how.
> (Ms. Quan Holden)

A third Board member made only a token, but
positive, reference to the MHP.

> Mr. G., a White educator who had been active
> in local San Francisco politics, stated that if
> the college could afford tennis courts, it
> could certainly afford to subsidize mental
> health services. (Ms. Quan Holden)

There was no direct or privileged communication
between the Board of Governors and the MHP administrators until 1974. However, the three members who spoke

in favor of the MHP in 1972 appeared to bode well for the long-range prospects of the program.

V

THE MENTAL HEALTH PROGRAM, 1974-76

Shifts in the Administrative Structure and Sponsorship of the Mental Health Program

During the last several months of 1973 and the early months of 1974, a contract with Progress Foundation of San Francisco was negotiated and implemented in order for that agency to assume sponsorship of the MHP. The process by which the transfer of sponsorship took place was somewhat fortuitous.

Progress Foundation (PF) was an agency which administered halfway houses for the emotionally disturbed. Although PF had been a member agency of the WCMHS consortium, there had been no formal administrative link between the MHP and PF, other than their common membership as "sister" agencies of the consortium. Following numerous unsuccessful attempts to gain an agency sponsor, PF was mentioned as a possible MHP auspices in a casual conversation I had with the WCMHS Executive Director. Since I knew its Medical Director through my private psychotherapy practice as a close professional colleague, it was suggested that PF might be a "natural" as a sponsoring agency. Also, PF was already a well respected WCMHS agency and, therefore, would not encounter obstacles in qualifying as an acceptable aegis for the MHP.

Shortly after this discussion with the WCMHS Executive Director, I entered into very informal, bilateral talks with the Medical Director of PF, which resulted in a preliminary agreement to place the MHP under PF sponsorship, pending the approval of the Board of Directors of PF.

> I was eager to offer PF as a sponsor for the MHP since an administrative umbrella was desperately needed. You needed a good liaison organization and the MHP was the kind of program which PF was already prepared to take care of. You were pushed out of CMCP and would possibly fold without an organizational sponsor. Also, for me personally, the MHP meant a great deal. I had been involved in other college psychological services and was deeply concerned with the mental health needs of college students. I knew you and I could communicate and work well together, so there were no reservations on that score. I also quickly realized that the college administration and Board of Governors did not truly understand the psychological needs of students. In my opinion, their attitude was, "We have a business to run and the mental health needs of students are not our responsibility." PF could spontaneously tune in to the gap between needs and services which the MHP was bridging. No other program at City College, certainly not the Counseling Department, was dealing appropriately with the acute psychological needs of students. Thus, our ready of-

144

fer of sponsorship.
(Medical Director, Progress Foundation)

The sponsorship proposal was placed before the
PF Board of Directors and quickly received its reso-
lute support.

> We (the PF Board of Directors) did not want to
> see the MHP go under. You and our Medical Di-
> rector knew each other well. She vouched for
> you; your program would certainly not be an
> embarrassment to PF. The Board unanimously
> and enthusiastically voted for sponsorship.
> Several factors were paramount to this deci-
> sion: (1) Since you and the Medical Director
> had a close, positive professional relationship,
> the adoption of the MHP seemed more like a per-
> sonal agreement than a cold business deal. This
> made it all the more palatable; (2) There seemed
> to be little administrative work or time re-
> quired to oversee the MHP, which was a plus; and
> (3) One of our Board members had once served
> as a trainee in the MHP. He strongly praised
> and recommended it to the rest of the Board,
> on the basis of his personal experience. This
> carried great weight with the Board. We at PF
> wanted to see the MHP ultimately adopted by the
> college. I considered the college administra-
> tion's opposition to adopting the MHP as a per-
> sonal battle, led by the Chancellor-Superin-
> tendent, which had little to do with the qual-
> ity or value of the services which the MHP
> provided to students.
> (Managing Director, Progress Foundation)

Under the terms of the contract which was negotiated with PF, the Medical Director provided two
hours per week of psychiatric consultation to the
MHP staff. She met with the staff in order to evaluate the quality of their clinical work, provide psychotherapeutic recommendations and, when appropriate,
prescribe psychotropic medications.

145

Within the context of the PF organization, the management and auditing of funds and the administration of liaison activities with the college administration and other community agencies were largely the responsibility of two administrative directors: the PF Executive Director and the Managing Director. Since there continued to be WCMHS funding of the MHP, the MHP remained a member agency of the WCMHS consortium.

From the advent of their sponsorship of the MHP, the administrators and the Board of Directors of PF were wholehearted and active backers of the college program.

> The PF staff and Board were fantastic. They gave of their time generously and always treated us (the staff of the MHP) with the utmost respect. They stood by us throughout many crises and proved to be unflinching allies against the adversaries of our program. It was a wonderful thing: dealing with such a decent and reasonable group of people.
> (Ms. Quan Holden)

Positive Identification Between the Mental Health Program and Progress Foundation

In undergoing a transfer of administrative authority to PF, the MHP, as the "change target," developed what Shein (1969) calls "positive identification with its new organizational sponsor. The conditions which Shein (1969) considers essential to a positive identification between a change target

146

(the MHP and its change agent (PF) were unmistakably
stamped upon the relationship between the MHP and PF.

> (1) Target is free to leave situation; (2) tar-
> get takes role voluntarily; (3) agent does not
> necessarily occupy formal role; (4) target
> experiences autonomy, sense of power, and
> choice; (5) target experiences trust and
> faith in agent; (6) target can terminate
> change process. (p. 107)

The above-mentioned organizational ingredients
were evident throughout the tenure of the relationship
between the MHP and PF. Thus, the PF sponsorship could
aptly be described as a "wonderful thing."

The Quest for Funding

In the Spring semester, 1974, the college administration, mainly through its primary spokesman to the
MHP, the Dean of Students, indicated that the college
would not deviate from its policy of providing only
matching funds to support the continuance of the MHP.
In other words, basic funding would have to first be
secured from other governmental and private resources
before the college could enter the funding picture.
Since Zellerbach Family Foundation, Bothin Helping
Fund and WCMHS all forecasted an expiration of their
funding of the MHP (the "demonstration" project had
successfully demonstrated its value to the host institution and each of the funding agencies, therefore,
refused to subsidize a program which they regarded as

147

finally the fiscal responsibility of the Community College District), the MHP was once again faced with the imminent prospect of financial insolvency and dissolution.

In response to this threat to the integrity of the MHP, several diverse and concurrent administrative tacks were taken: (1) Passionate appeals were made to the agencies which were already funding the MHP, explaining that their financial withdrawal spelled the demise of the program; (2) An application for funding was submitted to San Francisco County Mental Health Services; (3) Applications for subsidizations were mailed throughout the nation to scores of private foundations; and (4) An appeal was made to the President of City College to consider restoring the funds which were soon to expire, by increasing the college allocation to the MHP to $60,000.

Appeals to Current Funding Agencies

The desperation and humility with which I applied to the Bothin Helping Fund for refunding of the MHP are apparent in the following letter.

> In light of the prospective expiration of foundation support, we were notified by the college district that it will reduce its allocation proportionately. This, in turn, has the domino effect of reducing or eliminating our federal matching funds (WCMHS had not yet finalized its decision to defund the MHP).

In short, our program is faced with the prospect of dissolution at the end of August, 1974. I realize that Bothin Helping Fund has already been extremely generous in supporting the MHP. Therefore, I hope you will not think me too presumptuous if I again turn to you for continuance of your support, but the desperateness of our situation leaves me no alternative. I hope it is possible that you could allocate $15,000 a year for the next two years. It seems probable that by 1976 there will be legislative or fiscal breakthroughs which will enable our program to be self-supporting and secure. Much of our effort between now and then will be devoted to that objective.

About a month later, I received the following letter from the Executive Director of Bothin Helping Fund.

I sincerely regret having to inform you that the Bothin Helping Fund is not in a position to grant the request required for your program. We wish it were possible to fund the many worthwhile projects that come to our attention; however, the many demands upon our available funds dictate responses which are adverse to our sincere interest. We do regret this decision and hope that you will find some means to carry on your program.

An application for refunding the MHP was submitted to the Zellerbach Family Fund. The reply from its Executive Director reads as follows:

I have had a chance to review your proposal and to take a look at your 1974-75 budget. I appreciate your commitment to the program and your wish to see it continue to move ahead. It is not going to be possible for me to secure funds to continue our support. There are a number of organizations that we are involved with whose existence is threatened and where we are a major source of support. Your budget is far from plush and more likely shoestring.

149

It seems to me that you need to continue to
secure your growth funds from City College
now that you are accepted as a budget item.
I am sorry for this turndown and hope that
you understand that there continues to be enthusiasm for the program and the service your
staff offers.

In June, 1974 the Executive Director of the

WCMHS reported the decision of his agency relative to

my application for a continuance of WCMHS funding of

the MHP.

I regret to inform you that the recommendation
to the Board of Directors will be that Westside
not fund the City College Mental Health Program
in fiscal year 1974/75. As you know, Westside
has supported your program at City College
since January of 1970. There have been attempts,
though unsuccessful, to have other community
health centers in San Francisco participate in
the funding of the City College Mental Health
Program. Since 1972, the Community College
District has also put funds into your program.
Our recommendation for non-funding is based on
the sincere hope that the San Francisco Community College District will view mental health
services at City College as a viable and important service. If so, then it will appear that
now is the time for the Community College District to totally budget for the Mental Health
Program. I can assure you that the concept of
the City College project being totally funded
by the Community College District has Westside's
support at both the Board of Directors' level
and the Community Advisory Board's level.

Although the original funding agencies were un-

able to continue their financial assistance to the MHP,

they each gave strong organizational support to the

permanence of the MHP. Their encouragement to secure

additional funding from the Community College District

was undoubtedly a spur to my attempts to attain that very objective.

The San Francisco County Mental Health Service

In the Spring semester, 1974, the Dean of Students informed me that the Chancellor-Superintendent had recommended that an application be submitted to the San Francisco County Mental Health Services (SFCMHS), for funding of the MHP. I was told that the Chancellor-Superintendent would exercise his considerable influence with the SFCMHS administration to shepherd the application successfully through the county organization.

In addition to the earlier-mentioned reservations I held about a county administered MHP, my interest in this plan was further dampened by well publicized reports in the mental health community that the county was not adopting more adjunctive programs due to its own financial infirmities. Nevertheless, I readily corresponded with the Program Chief of the SFCMHS, informing him of the fiscal plight of the MHP and eliciting the assistance of his agency.

I was then advised by the Dean of Students to compose a "County Plan Report" according to the guidelines which the county issued for grant applications.

This report was signed by the City College President
and transmitted to the Director of the State Department
of Health in Sacramento, California. It contained the
following key proposal.

> The following is a proposal for funding from
> each San Francisco Community Mental Health
> Center for the academic year, September 1974 to
> August 1975. We believe this funding arrange-
> ment would be equitable since it is based upon
> mental health intake figures for each district
> served and will realistically replace the fund-
> ing that terminates in June, 1974.

#1 Mission	25%$30,000 =	$7,500
#2 Westside	17%$30,000 =	5,000
#3 Bayview/Hunters Point	7%$30,000 =	2,100
#4 Northeast	13%$30,000 =	3,900
#5 Sunset/Richmond	37%$30,000 =	11,100
		$29,700
Out of San Francisco + 1% outside		300
		$30,000

Copies of this report were sent to members of
the San Francisco Board of Supervisors and to the central office of the SFCMHS. The Dean of Students then
requested that I attend, with him, a San Francisco
Board of Supervisors meeting on county mental health
services in order to voice my advocacy of the MHP directly to the local legislators. The Supervisors, at
this meeting, were largely preoccupied with the alleged
maladministration of the Northeast Mental Health Services, and there was neither time nor inclination to
entertain discussion on other matters. The Dean of
Students and I were strictly spectators at this meeting.

I was then requested, by a county official, to present my grant application to the SFCMHS Health Advisory Board. During my presentation, a San Francisco County Supervisor, Mr. L., who served as a Board of Supervisors liaison to the Health Advisory Board, expressed concern for the future of the MHP. Mr. L. advised me to send him materials which could assist him in analyzing and evaluating the status of the MHP. Since Mr. L. was a well known and influential legislator, I stressed in my report to him the legislative gaps and deficiencies which were adversely affecting the MHP.

> There are no provisions in the educational code which require the institution of mental health services on the California community college campuses. The code is permissive and allows for the establishment of such services when practicable. The provisions which do require personal or health services restrict such programs to medical services or academic counseling. These programs, although vital to students, are basically not oriented or equipped to deal with many of the severe emotional problems with which college students must frequently cope. A competent psychiatric staff which is prepared to deal with emotional crises in an intensive and therapeutic manner, immediately and confidentially, is an absolute necessity to large numbers of community college students. The fact that the educational codes do not acknowledge this is a glaring and tragic omission.

About two months later, I received the following letter from Supervisor L.

I have not forgotten the discussion at the Men-

tal Health Advisory meeting nor your letter
and enclosures regarding the mental health
program at City College. Please forgive me
for not responding sooner. Since the provision of health services for California community colleges is set forth in the state
education code, I am not certain what action
can be taken by the San Francisco Board of
Supervisors to include mental health services.
I would be interested in hearing what steps
you think could be taken on a local level to
to institute such services, and I welcome your
ideas.

In a subsequent telephone conversation, Supervisor L. sympathetically indicated that he possessed
no political leverage to effect legislative changes
on the state level in behalf of the MHP, nor could
he raise support for the proposal for county funding
since the prospects of that plan would depend upon
fiscal determinations made in a state office outside
his jurisdiction.

Following on the heels of Supervisor L.'s dis-
mal communication, the SFCMHS notified me of its unqualified rejection of the grant application. The
application was denied on vague grounds, having to
do with "programmatic priorities, rising operational
costs and state-wide and local funding cutbacks."
Despite a considerable expenditure of professional
time and energy in prusuing the "County Plan," this
administrative tack was devoid of substantive value
to the MHP.

Grant Applications to Private Foundations

The first step in applying for private foundation funding of the MHP, was to consult local and national foundation directories, with the aim of as-
certaining the purpose, activities and locations of
the respective foundations. Foundations in California, particularly those in the San Francisco Bay
Area, were saturated with applications and materials
about the MHP. More geographically distant foundations
were selected as grant targets when there seemed to
be likelihood that the MHP fell within the purview
of the foundation. Transcribing and mailing the
grant applications was an enormously time-consuming
activity, since the proposals were varied according
to the stated goals of each foundation. For example,
the grant application to Weight Watchers Foundation,
Inc. contained a proposal to study and evaluate
psychotherapeutic services with obese college students.

With the exception of two woefully inappreciable
grants, all of the scores of grant applications to private foundations were flatly denied.

Two typical replies are here included.

Although yours is a very commendable program,
the trustees of Copley Charities regret their

> inability to offer funds. Existing pledge
> commitments make it impossible to approve ad-
> ditional grants, even within the geographic
> areas served by Copley Newspapers.

> The Board of Directors of the Louis R. Lurie
> Foundation thoroughly discussed your propo-
> sal. The conclusion of the Directors was that
> your request does not fall within the funding
> concepts of the Foundation at this time.

In one instance I received a telephone call
from a local foundation to notify me that its funding
deadline was that very evening, at which time the
board would convene to make its grant determinations.
I was asked to supplement the application I had submitted with additional materials about the MHP. I
drove to the foundation office in downtown San Francisco, arriving 15 minutes before the board meeting.
The next day I was informed that the proposal was,
with regret, denied.

In two separate grants, the MHP received a
total of $600 as a result of its entire solicitation
of private foundations. One hundred dollars was contributed as a gift by relatives of a personal friend
who were associated with a New York foundation. A
grant of $500 was made by the Peter Haas Fund of San
Francisco, after several letters and phone calls were
made to its President.

We are pleased to send the enclosed contribu-

156

tion to help in the funding of the Mental Health
Program at City College. The extensive demands
on our funds made it extremely difficult to
include this new allocation; in fact it was
done largely in view of your follow-through
and dedication to the program.
(President, Peter Haas Fund)

An Application for Funding from the Community College District

The failure to raise monies from its former
funding agencies, the SFCMHS and private foundations
left the MHP with only one viable alternative: to disregard the official dictum of the college administration that it would provide only matching funds and to
apply for a twofold increase (from $30,000 to $60,000)
in the college district allocation for the MHP. When
this intention was mentioned to the Dean of Students,
it was gainsaid because it violated previous agreements
and contracts. I told the Dean of Students that the
historical precedents for financially operating the MHP
had no bearing on the present crisis and then proceeded to file the following application with the
City College President.

I am submitting a budget request of $60,000 to
finance the Mental Health Program for the academic year 1974-75. It has become evident that
no financial resources are available to the
Mental Health Program, other than the Community College District itself. Since the funds
which we are seeking to underwrite the MHP
would come exclusively from the College Dis-

157

trict, we are also seeking approval for adoption of the program by the College District, i.e., that all Mental Health staff become full-status employees of the college.

The President responded to my proposal in the following memorandum:

This is to inform you that: 1. Your budget request of $60,000 to finance the Mental Health Program for the academic year 1974-75 has been denied. Funding will continue as per the matching agreement of 1973-74. 2. Staffing plans for the Student Health Services for 1974-75 will not include the hiring of mental health staff as full status employees of the Community College District. The most appropriate method for continuing the program during the next year would be to arrange for a contract with an outside agency, preferably Westside.

The MHP was caught in what is colloquially described as a Catch-22. The college would willingly match funds; however, there were no funds available for matching purposes. Therefore, the offer of the college district to provide funds on a matching basis only was meaningless and indicative of a hopeless obliviousness on the part of the college administration to the financial realities of the MHP.

In hastily organized conferences, Ms. Quan Holden and I planned several strategems to deal with the critical situation. The first was a letter campaign throughout the City College campus. Each faculty member received the following letter.

We need your help! Since its inception in

1970, the City College Mental Health Program
has been funded and sponsored by private foundations and the Westside Mental Health Services.
Since 1972 the Community College District has
subsidized about 50% of mental health costs.
From 1970 to the present about 2,000 different
students have been provided individual and
group psychotherapy. Mental Health staff provided about 4,800 hours of service to these
2,000 students. Because foundation and federal funds were originally used for demonstration purposes, they are due to expire in August
1974. The future success of the Mental Health
Program depends upon: (1) The Community College District restoring the private and the
federal funds which have expired and (2) The
Community College District adopting the Mental Health Program by hiring its current staff,
most of whom have served on this campus three
years.

The faculty were exhorted to attend the Board of Gov-

ernors' meeting at which the above-mentioned proposal

would be submitted. Also, all letters of endorsement

sent to the Board of Governors were appreciated.

Virtually the same letter which the faculty re-

ceived was also sent to the staffs and Board of Direc-

tors of the WCMHS, PF, Zellerbach Family Fund and Bothin

Helping Fund. The Counseling Department at City College

was also requested to recommend the MHP to the college

administration. It did so in a memorandum to the Presi-

dent:

The Counseling Department of City College recommends that appropriate steps be taken to insure
the maintenance of the Mental Health Clinic on
the campus on a continuing basis. The loss of
the clinic would be a damaging loss to the students of City College.

159

The day after the campus was inundated with MHP solicitations for faculty support, I was called into the Dean of Students' office and berated for "embarrassing the President. This type of tactic makes him look foolish; going behind his back." I stated that I did not believe the letter drive was an embarrassment to the President since no mention was made of him or his role in the matter. (This reply was disingenuous. There obviously was a risk of causing the President embarrassment by mobilizing the faculty to rally behind a proposal which he had just denied. It was a risk that Ms. Quan Holden and I felt had to be taken, considering the dire conditions overshadowing the MHP.) I quickly arranged to see the President, who had not yet seen the letters which had been sent to the faculty. I explained my reasons (sheer desperation) for taking such measures and apologized for any embarrassment I may have caused him. He responded stoically to my comments and indicated that he foresaw no serious problems arising out of the episode.

It is necessary to digress here in order to mention an administrative change in the college which had great relevancy for the MHP. In the Spring of 1974, the President had tendered his resignation in order to assume the superintendency of another community college

160

district. Although he was not an active supporter of the MHP, he was generally considered by the MHP staff to be a fair, candid and competent administrator. He was a fiscal conservative, particularly in relation to service programs such as the MHP, yet his posture toward the MHP had been generous (as evidenced by the $30,000 allocation). In his administrative dealings with the MHP staff, his manner was considerate and equanimous.

> The major concern about the MHP during my tenure as President of City College was whether the program was duplicating already existing resources in the community. Despite concerns on that score, it became evident that the MHP was not duplicating community services. My assessment of the MHP was that it was providing high-quality psychological services to students. There was a degree of apprehension at the college that the institution of the MHP would constitute a jurisdictional invasion of the Counseling Department. With the exception of a very few counselors, that problem did not materialize. I suppose one of my main worries was whether the health service would need to resort to student health fees in order to remain in operation. I saw such fees as the precursors of tuition. I'm philosophically opposed to tuition and believe it is more difficult to argue against tuition once fees are imposed on students. At the time I was leaving the college I believe the Chancellor-Superintendent had a close working relationship with the administrators of the County Mental Health Services. I think he had hoped to capitalize on that relationship by gaining county support for the MHP. I don't know how that eventually worked out.
> (Former President, City College)

Following the resignation of the City College

President, a man who had formerly served as Dean of Business Affairs was appointed interim President of the college. The administrative negotiations which took place between the interim President and the MHP will be discussed later in this chapter.

Because the President had already submitted his resignation, Ms. Quan Holden and I viewed his incumbency, to a considerable extent, as a "lame duck." This was one reason we did believe he would not be seriously victimized by the controversy which our lobbying would foment. This factor may also account for the President's unusual equanimity in handling the letter campaign.

The final step in gathering support for total funding and adoption of the MHP by City College was to contact City College Governor S. Governor S. expressed immediate interest in supporting the proposal for full ($60,000) college funding of the MHP. He was more irresolute over the matter of integrating the program into the college system. He indicated that the Board of Governors never hired particular personnel and that a resolution to adopt the MHP positions *per se*, would require board votes which were perhaps "not there." He requested that I send him information which would clarify the nature of the proposal and agreed to spearhead the application for adequate funding of the MHP in the forthcoming Board of Governors meeting.

At the June Board of Governors meeting, Mr. S. submitted a resolution to grant the MHP $60,000 for the academic year, 1974-75.

> I thought his presentation was somewhat diffuse. Although he made it clear that the $60,000 allocation was essential, he seemed to equivocate when it came to the matter of college adoption of the MHP. He appeared not to want to go out on a limb over that one. (Ms. Quan Holden)

The outcome of the Board of Governors meeting was a renewal of the contract between City College and PF, based upon an allocation of $60,000, to maintain the MHP for one more academic year. The MHP no longer held membership in the WCMHS consortium since WCMHS funds no longer supported the program. Following the meeting, I was informed that the MHP had generated the greatest outpouring of letters of endorsement in the entire history of the Community College District. This was all the more remarkable since many instructors had already left the campus in June, except for brief returns in order to administer final examinations to students.

Theoretical Considerations

The quest for MHP funding brought into focus

some of the distinguishing characteristics of the authoritarian nature of the college administration. As
Watson (1969) suggests, authoritarian administrations
manifest a proclivity to resist change in social systems. They do so by an excessive conformity to norms,
a preoccupation with vested interests, a view of tradi-
tions as being sacrosanct and by a xenophobic rejection
of outsiders.

The MHP inspired the college administration's
antagonism and opposition by virtue of the following:
(1) It was a facility administered by "outsiders" who
were becoming a major impetus for change in the host
institution. Despite the suspicions which the "outsider" status engendered, the college administration resolved to solidify that status by refusing to adopt the
MHP, thereby justifying and reinforcing its distrust.

(2) The historical precedents for funding the
MHP were regarded by the Dean of Students as inviolable
and sacrosanct. The MHP's success in producing new
(internal) methods of raising funds was distrusted,
partly because the methods themselves departed from
traditional means of financially maintaining the program.

(3) The vested interest of the college administration was to minimize costs and maximize educational

164

benefits. At the time of the inception of the MHP in 1970, the spread between costs and benefits was pronounced, since the MHP derived no funds from the college. When the college became the sole subsidizer of the MHP, the college administration perceived the narrowing of the gap between costs and benefits as a threat to its vested interest: another basis for opposing the actions of the MHP administrators.

(4) By eliciting faculty and community support for the MHP, the MHP administrators were breaching norms which were immensely important to the college administration, i.e., that all administrative efforts to achieve programmatic objectives must follow officially established channels of communication and authority. The MHP had violated a time-honored norm: conformity to administrative authority. Non-conformity was perhaps a more serious dynamic in arousing the Dean of Students' ire than the anticipated embarrassment of the President.

Adorno, *et al.* (1950) found that,

The authoritarian personality defends against his fear of authority by the psychological mechanism of projection. Thus it is not oneself but others that are seen as hostile and threatening. Or else one's weakness leads to an exaggerated condemnation of everything that is weak; one's own weakness is thus fought outside instead of inside. As long as social conditions are conducive to and furnish ac-

ceptable outlets for compensatory tendencies,
a relative mental balance within the individual
may well be achieved.

The Dean of Students, who straightforwardly represented the policies of his administrative superordinates, could not acknowledge that those policies were
inimical to the welfare of the MHP. As his administrative subordinate, striving from a position of relative weakness to maintain the MHP, I was criticized
for being hostile and threatening to the authority of
the President. My weakness, not the Dean of Students',
in dealing with the policies of his administrative
superiors, was a cause for condemnation. By disrup-
ting and altering the social conditions of the college,
namely the hierarchical system of determining the status of service programs, I was also undermining the
"mental balance" of those administrators for whom the
unorthodox methods of the MHP were ego-alien.

A Meeting with the Chancellor-Superintendent

In the early Fall, 1974 Ms. Quan Holden and I
received disquieting indications from the Dean of Students that the Chancellor-Superintendent intended to
arrange for SFCMHS sponsorship and funding of the MHP
for the academic year, 1974-75. I went to see the
Chancellor-Superintendent in order to verify the Dean's

statements and, if necessary, to deter him from his
designs upon the MHP. I was told categorically that
the MHP would, the following year, be integrated into
the SFCMHS system or it would be liquidated. He explained that such programs were the administrative and
fiscal responsibility of expert agencies such as SFCMHS,
not the community college. He implacably refused to
reconsider his decision. I was advised to reconcile
myself to his plan to integrate the MHP into the county
system. The fate of the MHP was sealed, non-negoti-
able and utterly at the mercy of the Chancellor-Superintendent. In painstaking deliberations, following
my conference with the Chancellor-Superintendent, Ms.
Quan Holden and I decided to do all within our power,
privately and publicly, to refute and crush the Chancellor-Superintendent's plans for the MHP. Two strategies were framed. One strategy was to lobby the
Board of Governors in order to convince them to for-
sake the Chancellor-Superintendent in his ambitions
for the MHP. The second strategy was two-pronged:
to outwit and impede those college administrators who
would obligingly seek to implement the Chancellor-
Superintendent's plan in our intramural dealings with
them and in our public relations activities with the
off-campus community.

Lobbying the Board of Governors

Our first step was for Ms. Quan Holden to visit City College Governor D., a local banker who had heretofore not expressed himself on the subject of the MHP in Board meetings. He was selected as an early recipient of our lobbying because he was Asian, and since Ms. Quan Holden was also Asian, it was hoped that their ethnic commonality might produce an important alliance.

> He was initially very much the "company man." I explained the difficulties facing the MHP, described the drawbacks of the Chancellor-Superintendent's plan and asked for his support. He displayed little knowledge of the intricacies of the problems confronting the MHP, actually seemed somewhat indifferent to them and finally indicated that he would adhere to whatever the college administration recommended. (Ms. Quan Holden)

Ms. Quan Holden and I then decided to survey other City College Governors in order to assess their attitudes toward the status of the MHP. Phone calls were made to Governors S., C., a White educator, G. and E., a White former President of City College. "Governor X. was initially rather rushed and inaccessible. My two calls to her were largely non-productive" (Ms. Quan Holden).

Eventually, Governors X. and C. encouraged me to speak with them in person at an upcoming faculty association reception, without volunteering personal opinions about our concerns. Governor E. was only briefly available to talk with me due to illness in his family. He indicated, matter-of-factly, that my calls were unnecessary since he would evaluate the status of the MHP on the basis of discussions with the Chancellor Superintendent (Governor E. and the Chancellor-Superintendent were close and long-time personal friends who had worked together in the administrative ranks of City College for many years).

In response to my call, Governor G. was even more circumspect. He immediately requested information about the opinions of other Governors towards the MHP. Although sympathetic to our request for assistance, he was unwilling to hazard an exprssion of his own views on the administrative difficulties of the MHP.

At the faculty association reception I vocalized to Governors X. and C. my doubts and criticisms of the Chancellor-Superintendent's plan for the MHP. Both Governors seemed friendly to the concept of a college-sponsored MHP; however, their intentions relative to the MHP were obscure. It is not unimportant that the discussions with the two Governors were held in a public milieu at a time when the Chancellor-Superintendent was in attendance. Observing me confer with the Governors, he mimicked my behavior by hold-

ing up a hand and flapping four fingers against the
thumb, as if to mark me a yapper.

The first round of lobbying the Board of Governors, in an attempt to defeat the "County Plan," was
inauspicious and disheartening. Ms. Quan Holden and I
then resolved to undertake our lobbying in a more intensive, thorough, systematic and sophisticated manner.
We again attempted to enlist Governor S. in organizing the Board of Governors to renounce the County Plan.

> This time Governor S. was very reluctant to act.
> He told us that he didn't think the votes "were
> there" to sustain a resolution to adopt the MHP.
> Besides, he had been the principal champion of
> the MHP in the past. He thought it was now
> some other Board member's turn to bear the brunt
> of that responsibility. His general attitude
> had changed. He was almost unfriendly. Per-
> haps he was beginning to feel manipulated. Or
> perhaps he had other irons in the fire and didn't
> want to use his political chips on a cause like
> the MHP. (Ms. Quan Holden)

Mr. S. stated to me that he might be willing
to consider "supporting" a resolution to adopt the MHP,
but only if there were definitely sufficient votes for
ratification. "Do you have the necessary votes?,"
he asked. "I think so," I replied, listing the Governors who appeared supportive. "That's not good enough.
You must know for certain." I was then in an insoluble quandary. "How can I know for certain? No Governor is going to make such an absolute pledge, at least

certainly not to me." He indicated, not apathetically, that I would have to find out exactly what the various Governors intended to decide about the MHP and then report my findings to him.

At about this time, in the Spring of 1975, Governor E. resigned from the board. Ms. Quan Holden and I regarded his resignation as a boon to the MHP since there seemed to be no possibility of driving a philosophical wedge between Governor E. and the Chancellor-Superintendent. Soon after Governor E.'s retirement, the Mayor of San Francisco appointed a Chicano realtor-social service director, Mr. B., to fill the board vacancy. I immediately sent Governor B. the following letter.

> First, allow me to congratulate you upon your appointment to the San Francisco Community College Board of Governors. As Director of the City College Mental Health Program, I thought it appropriate to forward the enclosed materials (published journal articles about the MHP) which might help to familiarize you with our campus service. At the next Board meeting I will be making a presentation which will address the subject of the future of the Mental Health Program. This subject has been a source of considerable Board discussion since the inception of our program in 1970. Hopefully, a resolution of our uncertain status can be achieved at the Board meeting. I naturally would be pleased to either meet or chat with you on the phone at any time regarding this matter.

Our next move was to scour the City College cam-

pus for an ally who personally knew Governor B. and who
would be willing to participate with us in a meeting
with him. We quickly ascertained that a Latino instructor, a President of the local chapter of the American Federation of Teachers (AFT) and an enthusiastic
friend of the MHP, had had personal and positive dealings with Governor B. He readily accompanied us to
Governor B.'s office for a conference.

> This was a helpful and encouraging conference.
> Although Governor B. was neophyte Board member
> who did not yet even have voting power, he dem-
> onstrated a quick and intelligent grasp of the
> issues and generally seemed empathic. He was
> receptive to discussing the matter further with
> other Board members and encouraged us to remain
> in close consultation with him. (Ms. Quan Holden)

Ms. Quan Holden and I then called Governors X.
and S., to request that we hold a meeting in order to
discuss the matter of the MHP's future in detail.
They both agreed to meet in Governor S.'s law office.
With Governor S.'s permission, I called Governor B.
to invite him to the meeting which was to take place
that afternoon. He indicated that he would attend
the meeting only if he received a direct verbal invitation from Governor S. to do so, since as a new
Board Governor it might be considered presumptuous of
him to insinuate himself into the meeting. I then
called Governor S. who was not then available. I

172

left a message for him to call Governor B. in order to extend a request to the latter to attend the meeting.

Ms. Quan Holden and I had, over the past several months, developed a close and highly supportive relationship with a Black City College instructor who was Chairperson of the Personnel Committee of the Academic Senate. He had had several positive interactions with Governor X. and, therefore, offered to assist us in the forthcoming meeting.

> The meeting started on an unfavorable note. Governor B. was not invited to the meeting by Governor S. Governor X. arrived over an hour late and didn't explain her tardiness to anyone. Governor S. was obviously angry and resentful. He accused you of manipulating him by leaving messages for him to call other Board members. You apologized, explaining that the exigencies of the moment required hurried decisions which were often clumsy and careless. He shot back, "You know perfectly well what you're doing. You've certainly not been careless or stupid." He appeared to be unpropitiable. Governor X. was also problematic. She indicated that she needed more time to make comparative studies of college mental health programs. The Personnel Committee Chairperson seemed to have no influence with her with respect to the MHP. Neither Governor seemed to want the burden of fighting for this controversial program. Also, I had the distinct impression that the ostensible need for comparative studies was a "red herring." It seemed that there were hidden, perhaps political reasons for the hesitancy over supporting us. (Ms. Quan Holden)

Ms. Quan Holden went to see Governor D. for the third time, at his bank office.

> I took the tack with him of describing the Coun-
> ty Plan as the Chancellor-Superintendent's vehi-
> cle for bringing in outsiders to do work which
> we (the insiders) had done for over five years.
> I also appealed to his "Asian" esteem for the
> family unit, by mentioning my child and your
> children. He began to budge by indicating that
> he would not want us to lose our jobs to un-
> known outsiders. (Ms. Quan Holden)

Through her research Ms. Quan Holden found that
there were two persons in the Chinatown community who
might be particularly influential with Governor D.-- a
prominent local judge and the priest of Governor D.'s
church.

> I went to see the judge in his chambers. I had
> to leave momentarily and when I returned he was
> gone. I left a message which explained our sit-
> uation and requested his intercession. I don't
> know whether he actually interceded. I then
> went to see Governor D.'s priest who promised to
> speak with Governor D. I called the priest af-
> terward. He indicated that he had spoken with
> Governor D., although it wasn't possible to as-
> sess the impact of this assistance. (Ms. Quan
> Holden)

Ms. Quan Holden and I together went to see Governor D. two more times.

> By the time we had seen him twice more, Governor
> D. seemed to be quite conversant with the issues
> and was pronouncing his opposition to the County
> Plan. He decidedly favored our continuance in
> the MHP because he felt our dedicated service
> merited such support. (Ms. Quan Holden)

Ms. Quan Holden and I made several forays to gain
the support of Governor F., a White attorney. After
trying to reach him several times by phone without suc-

cess, Governor F. called to tell me that he was not inclined, as a Board member, to do business with rank-
and-file college staff. His manner was brusque and
retentive.

Our research revealed that a clinical psychologist at Mt. Zion Hospital was a family relation of Governor F. I placed a call to this psychologist who a-
greed to recommend the MHP to Governor F. She was,
however, dubious about the prospects of altering Governor F.'s preconceptions or opinions about the MHP.

In discussing the dilemmas of the MHP with the
Executive Director of Zellerbach Family Fund, I discov-
ered that he had been a childhood friend of Governor
F.'s. He sent the following letter to Governor F.

> It has been a long time since we've met. I
> would like to put in a good word and a strong
> recommendation for the Mental Health Program
> at City College. The Zellerbach Family Fund
> was one of those who provided start-up funding
> in 1969. Over the past five years our total
> support has been close to $50,000. The spe-
> cial needs of many students at City College are
> met through this service. This foundation con-
> tinued to support the program beyond our regu-
> lar policy limit because the service was unique
> in setting a standard followed by other col-
> leges. I hope that the Board, even in these
> times of thin budgets, will provide for the
> full operation of the service.

A second psychologist, the Co-Director of the
Mt. Zion Crisis Clinic, reported that he knew well an
important local labor leader who probably had consid-

erable influence with Governor F. He called the labor
leader who, in turn, spoke to Governor F. in behalf of
the MHP.

The various statements of endorsement from
friends, relatives and professional associates with
which Governor F. was barraged appeared to have the
paradoxical effect of alienating him. "I called him
(Governor F.) and although he was not extremely un-
friendly, there seemed to be little chance to gain his
cooperation in helping us." (Ms. Quan Holden)

The lobbying of the Board of Governors was
deeply affected by a highly significant change in the
administrative leadership of the City College campus.
Late in the Spring semester, 1974, the City College
Board of Governors appointed a new President, a Black
counseling psychologist, who was recruited from outside the community college district. The principal
"in-house" candidate for the Presidency was the Acting
President, who was the favorite of many of the long-
standing administrative staff and of the Chancellor-
Superintendent.

> In support of the Acting President some of the
> high-ranking administrative staff (including
> the Dean of Students) distributed petitions to
> administrators and rank-and-file with which the
> signatories were to indicate their support of
> the appointment of the Acting President to the
> Presidency of the college. Presumably, those

176

> who did not sign the petition were placed on
> some kind of "shit-list" for further reference.
> On good authority it has been reported that
> when the Board of Governors rejected the Act-
> ing President, and in his stead appointed Presi-
> dent O., the Chancellor-Superintendent literally
> cried. (Chairperson, Personnel Committee, Fac-
> ulty Senate)

In my opinion, it was no coincidence that the administrative staff which circulated and backed the petition were almost exclusively White men with longevity on the campus. Their bias was to promote the candidacy of someone much like themselves (the Acting President) rather than a Black "outsider."

Soon after the appointment of President O., I called Governor G., who formerly had been circumspect and non-committal. I asked for his support in defeating the County Plan. He again wanted to know what "the others" (Board members) were doing. I told him that there appeared to be widespread support of the MHP among the Governors; however, it was possible that his would be a "swing" vote. For that reason it was essential that he support the adoption of the MHP. Governor G. did not declare his position on the County Plan, but in reference to the permanent adoption of the MHP, he made the following comments:

> Look, the Chancellor-Superintendent just took
> a kick in the ass over the appointment of Presi-
> dent O. I don't want to see him get kicked in
> the ass again by pushing through the adoption

of the MHP now. It's too soon to hit him again, after what he just went through.

I responded by angrily asking whether the community college district was being run for the welfare of the Chancellor-Superintendent. Governor G. apologized, stated again that the juxtaposition of the two issues (the appointment of President O. and the resolution of the status of the MHP) made it impossible for him to take a more affirmative position on the MHP. He advised me to wait one more year, at which time perhaps President O. would be in sufficient command to recommend an expeditious resolution of the administrative problems of the MHP.

Two final calls were made: to Governors C. and S. After trying unsuccessfully to reach Governor C. at his home for a week, I called his place of employment: a strategic error. Governor C. scolded me for invading his professional privacy. He was unamenable to discussing my purpose in calling him and abruptly halted our talk by indicating that he would be taking up the matter (of the MHP) with Governor S. (Governors S. and C. were generally considered to be philosophically compatible and mutually supportive Board members).

My last call to Governor S. was not reassuring. He asked if I had mustered sufficient Board votes to carry a resolution for college adoption of the MHP. I said that the votes *seemed* to "be there." He stated that my conjectural hopes were not good enough. He mentioned that the extent of Board support would most likely become crystallized in the closed Executive Session which immediately preceded the upcoming Board meeting. Perhaps, following the Executive Session, he would offer me a cue as to the Board's general position regarding the status of the MHP. I could then determine, on the basis of this intelligence, what course of action to take at the Board meeting itself.

Methods Used to Outwit and Impede College Administrators

In the Fall, 1974 Ms. Quan Holden and I were informed that the Acting Dean of Business Affairs (ADBA) was under instructions from the Chancellor-Superintendent to proceed with negotiations with the SFCMHS. Ms. Quan Holden and I requested, through the Dean of Students, that we be allowed to participate in these negotiations and were told that our involvement was unnecessary and unwelcomed. We learned that the negotiations were to be conducted primarily by the ADBA and the Clinical Assistant to the Program Chief of the SFCMHS. Despite administrative strictures relative to our involvement in the negotiations, I called the Clinical Assistant, whom I had known well professionally. I informed him of our objections to the County Plan. I also expressed my hope that the criticisms which we would level at the County Plan *per se* would not be interpreted as aspersions of the SFCMHS. He was sympathetic, but obviously in no position to refuse the college administration's (and his own Program Chief's) overture to evaluate seriously the feasibility of the County Plan.

The meeting between the ADBA and the Clinical Assistant are described as follows:

> The ADBA set the tenor of the meetings. Although he registered verbal support of the MHP, I felt that his support was shallow. I had the impression that there was an attempt to get out from under the MHP and that it was expedient to funnel funds through SFCMHS to give the MHP another administrative umbrella. Also, I felt that the ADBA had a personal problem with the MHP. I don't know what it was, but it seemed like there was an unspoken, irrational, almost retaliatory attitude toward the leadership of the MHP. Generally, there seemed to be an untrusting quality to the ADBA's opposition to the MHP. (Clinical Assistant to Program Chief, San Francisco Community Mental Health Services)

Following the consultations between the Clinical Assistant and the ADBA, I voiced objections to the Acting President over the exclusion of MHP personnel from the interagency negotiations. He indicated that we would be asked to directly assist the Clinical Assistant in evaluating the MHP and the County Plan and would eventually be fully informed of the county's findings and recommendations.

In the Spring of 1975, the Clinical Assistant undertook an evaluative study of the MHP.

> I didn't feel that it was a true professional evaluation. It might be described as a one-day assessment, a fact-finding mission. On the basis of my brief exposure to the MHP, I thought the clinical services were of a good quality. I liked the staff and there seemed to be a good flow to the program. The greatest morale factor was clearly the question of the survival of the program. The uncertainty surrounding that question, however, did not seem to impede the work of the staff. (Clinical Assistant to Program Chief, SFCMHS)

In a written report to the SFCMHS Program Chief, the Clinical Assistant referred to the quality of the MHP in the following respects:

> Charts up-to-date; show effective crisis techniques within a treatment framework that is largely psychoanalytic.
>
> Goals of therapy explicitly stated in charts.
>
> Students (clients) receive first interview in 1-3 days.
>
> Student trainees well integrated into the Mental Health Program.
>
> Excellent relationship between mental health and nursing staff located in same building.
>
> Morale good on staff except re. present funding uncertainties.
>
> Good staff and graduate student ethnic balance.
>
> Good peer supervision.

Excellent supervision to graduate students.

Low rate of clients who drop out of college seen in Mental Health Program as compared with student body as a whole. Needs further checking.

Public Relations

While awaiting the final recommendations of the SFCMHS, Ms. Quan Holden and I undertook public relations activities to gain added community and campus support for the MHP. I arranged to have the *San Francisco Chronicle* (1975) publish an article about a a survey of California's community colleges which I had recently learned had been accepted for publication in a professional journal.

Shortly after the appearance of the *San Francisco Chronicle* article I was interviewed on two radio stations regarding the findings of the survey. I then telephoned the UPI, which agreed to distribute the survey findings to newspapers statewide. Later in the Spring, a television station manager in Reading, California, who had read of the survey in a local newspaper, requested a television interview for his Reading station. Although the interview would not be aired on television for many months and would be seen only in a remote locale, it was hoped that it, along with the newspaper and radio publicity, would raise the stature of the MHP in the eyes of the San Francisco community and the City College Board of Governors.

Methods Used to Outwit and Impede College Administrators, Continued

Shortly following the newspaper publicity, I received a request from the ADBA to supply him with the raw data which had been used in the published survey. I readily conveyed the raw data to him, naively thinking that his interest was purely intellectual. I then became curious and called him for clarification. He stated that he wanted to test the validity of my findings. He was planning to consult independently with the various informants throughout the state's community colleges regarding the data which they had provided me. I told him that his intentions were reprehensible, since he had not discussed them openly with me. Furthermore, the integrity of my study was entirely defensible and needed none of his sleuthing for validation. He countered by stating that I had represented my findings to be scientific research and had used them to bolster the image of the MHP. Scientific research of this kind, from his point of view, required validation. My rejoinder was to point out

that there had never been a pretense that the study
was "scientific research." It was, rather, a survey
based upon opinions elicited from questionnaires.
I then excoriated him for planning a surreptitious
use of my data and flatly informed him that if he
chose to carry out his intentions, I would report the
matter to the appropriate authorities and charge him
with harassment and unethical professional conduct.
He immediately rescinded his plans to replicate my
study, and the matter was never brought up again.

Soon after the encounter with the ADBA, the
Dean of Students made several innuendoes to me about
the need to examine more carefully the ethnic balance
of the MHP, since affirmative action criteria would
be more seriously considered once the county assumed
sponsorship of the MHP. He indicated that I, in particular, might be jeopardized by the criteria because I was White. I informed him that my Spanish
surname and extraction, albeit the roots of which
stretched back many centuries, would enable me to
qualify in any test of affirmative action. Soon after this exchange I received a phone call from the
Dean. The call was, for the most part, unintelligible
since the Dean conversed with me in Spanish. I asked
for an interpretation and received only a light greet-

ing and advice to acquire a proficiency in Spanish.

Ms. Quan Holden and I next met with three representatives of the City College Student Council in
hopes of receiving an endorsement from that important elective group. The following is a letter from
the President of the Student Council to the Chancellor-Superintendent.

> As students on the City College campus, we
> are aware of the great need for mental health
> services on the campus. We feel that such
> services are important not only to our psycho-
> logical growth, but that they assist us tre-
> mendously in our academic endeavors. We have
> met with the administrative director and clin-
> inical coordinator of the Mental Health Program.
> The Student Council unanimously passed a motion
> to support the Mental Health Program's request
> for permanence by integration of it with the
> Student Health Service. The Student Health
> Service will insure that these services will
> be available to all students in our efforts
> at academic success.

Ms. Quan Holden reports the administration's

response to this letter:

> Shortly after registering their official en-
> dorsement of the MHP, the Student Council
> leaders were contacted by the Dean of Stu-
> dents. The Dean informed them that their ac-
> tions were premature, since they had not yet
> heard the other side (that of the college ad-
> ministration). The students told us laughingly
> that they then listened to the college admin-
> istration's side of the story, were impervious
> to it and had no regrets over their endorse-
> ment. They clearly regarded the administra-
> tion's tactics as attempts to pressure and in-
> timidate them.

I next called the Acting President to allege

that his minions were engaging in "underhanded" methods
of dealing with the MHP. I cited specifically the
tampering with the Student Council endorsement, the
Dean's conversation in Spanish and the ADBA's ferreting
out the raw data of the published survey. He remarked
that the MHP was producing the kind of controversy
which, regrettably, was leading to a bit of poor judgment. He hoped that all differences of opinion would
be reconciled and buried in future meetings between
the college administrators and the staff of the MHP.

A meeting was soon held. In attendance were
the Acting President, the Dean of Students, the ADBA,
the Coordinator of Student Health Services, Ms. Quan
Holden and I. We were informed that the county had
worked out the procedures and agreements to provide
the adminstrative umbrella for the MHP.

> We then asked to see the correspondence which
> contained the recommendations of the SFCMHS.
> The Acting President stated that the report was
> confidential and could not be imparted to us.
> You then, to their dismay, said that that was
> "disgraceful" since the Acting President had
> earlier promised to fully share the county's
> findings with us. At that point the Acting
> President requested the ADBA to retrieve the
> report from his office and read it to us. We
> were allowed to take notes on its contents,
> but not to receive a copy of it.
> (Ms. Quan Holden)

The earlier paragraphs of the letter prosa-
ically spelled out the mechanics of incorporating the

MHP into the SFCMHS. There was a proviso that an agency, such as Progress Foundation, be secured in order to sub-contract the MHP, since the SFCMHS, as a superagency, did not administer clinical programs itself. The last paragraph contained a key point which particularly excited our interest.

> I'm sure you understand that this proposed relationship between Community Mental Health Services and City College does not, from our position, imply any commitment that we will be in a position to fund any or part of the Mental Health Program in future years. We certainly do, however, believe that the on-campus delivery of mental health services is a key resource to students at City College whose academic aspirations are threatened by serious emotional problems.
> (Program Chief, San Francisco Community Mental Health Services)

The SFCMHS patently demonstrated in this letter that it had no long-range commitment to the MHP and would not contribute financially to its continuance in the future. Why then give it administrative rule over the MHP? The contents of this letter added appreciable weight to our argument against adoption of the County Plan. In one of my discussions with Governor S., I made a special point of informing him of the letter and its implications.

The ADBA and the Dean of Students next set out to negotiate an agreement with Progress Foundation to allow SFCMHS to sub-contract with Progress Foundation

187

for the continued administration of the MHP.

> The administrators of Progress Foundation, our
> solid allies, were constantly being informed by
> us of our opposition to the County Plan. Thus,
> they responded to the efforts of the college
> administration by being subtly obstructionist.
> They never committed themselves to agreeing to
> a sub-contract with the county. On the con-
> trary, when they were asked to take a posi-
> tion, they unfailingly supported the permanent
> integration of the MHP by the college. That
> must have been very frustrating for the college
> administration, since the success of the County
> Plan hinged on securing a community agency to
> sponsor the MHP. (Ms. Quan Holden)

In our consultation's with the administrators of

PF, Ms. Quan Holden and I counseled them not to refuse

outright to offer sponsorship of the MHP under county

auspices in the event that the Board of Governors ul-

timately passed the County Plan. We suggested, however,

that they leave the college administrators in consider-

able doubt as to their availability as an agency spon-

sor, in order to impair their confidence and effective-

ness in carrying out the County Plan. The PF admin-

istrators carried out their delicate assignment to

perfection.

Public Relations, Continued

In addition to the recognition the MHP received

in the media, Ms. Quan Holden and I, during the aca-

demic year 1974-75, were selected to serve on the

California Chancellor of Community Colleges' Ad Hoc

Health Services Committee. This committee was organized to evaluate the health needs of California's
community college students and to recommend health
programs to meet those needs. Although the Ad Hoc
Committee would not exert direct influence over the
events occurring on the City College campus, our membership on this prestigious committee (as its only
mental health practitioners -- the other members were
nurses and one dean) gave the MHP added importance as
an agency engaged in long-range, statewide health
planning.

One final measure which Ms. Quan Holden and I
successfully undertook was to secure an unqualified endorsement for college adoption of the MHP from the
Faculty Senate. This endorsement, from a campus organization which represented the entire college faculty, helped eliminate doubts as to the importance of the
MHP to the instructors of the college.

The Board of Governors Meeting, May 1975

In May, 1975 the MHP was, upon the request of
Ms. Quan Holden and me, placed on the agenda of the
meeting of the Board of Governors. Just prior to
the commencement of the Board meeting, I received a
message that Governor S. wished to speak with me. In

the privacy of a nearby office he informed me that there were not the requisite votes to sustain a resolution for college adoption of the MHP. Disconcertedly, I asked how he could be so sure. Perhaps he was mistaken. He said he was not mistaken. He added that this meant he would be submitting no resolutions to the Board that evening. "What should I do?" I asked. Governor S. said that was strictly my decision. But I should expect no support from the Board. Ms. Quan Holden and I quickly conferred and decided to go ahead with our petition to the Board for college adoption of the MHP. Perhaps Governor S. had underestimated the extent of Board support for such a resolution. Although our chances to immediately fulfill our greatest hopes were infinitesimal, there was little point in then reneging, since the MHP had already received a visible place on the Board agenda. Also, at some inconvenience to him, we had gained as a MHP spokesman for the evening the Chairperson of the Personnel Committee of the Academic Senate. In short, we did not want to waste an opportunity to further underscore and dramatize our appeal to the Board, even if we could not completely attain our objectives.

The Chairperson of the Personnel Committee of

the Academic Senate spoke in behalf of the Administrative Director and Clinical Coordinator of the MHP. He said that as long as City College is taking on new faculty members in the Fall, that these two people should also be taken on the permanent faculty in a program that has proven itself to be desirable and needed on the campus. The Chairperson feels that City College has a moral obligation to face up to the responsibility of accepting the MHP and to giving the Administrative Director and Clinical Coordinator full faculty status.

The Administrative Director of the MHP spoke regarding faculty status for himself and his assistant. He noted that this request does not imply expansion of the program nor increased allocations.

Governor G. said he would like to hear from administration in this respect.

The ADBA referred to his study on the MHP, copies of which had been furnished the Board. He feels that the issues are (1) the propriety of the San Francisco City College handling mental health services, and (2) how to best serve the students of the college without regard to specific personnel. The ADBA pointed out that the Program Chief of the SFCMHS has pledged that they would supply mental health services to the campus for a program in 1975-76 and, in order to develop a continuity of the program, would probably sub-contract with the same personnel presently involved. The Program Chief would also have his staff evaluate the program from the point-of-view of professionalism which the ADBA feels the college is not in a position to do. The ADBA recommended that the college contract with the SFCMHS for this program; however, he pointed out that there was no commitment on the part of the SFCMHS that they would definitely contract with the same personnel -- it was a verbal assurance only.

The Administrative Director of the MHP said he felt this proposal was preposterous -- he noted that the SFCMHS is presently under indictment from the State for the ineffective and costly

services it has been providing. (Minutes,
Board of Governors' Meeting, May, 1975)

Governor F.'s comments were formally prepared,
quite lengthy and seemed to serve as a nexus for the
ensuing discussion of the status of the MHP. Therefore, they are included comprehensively here, although
slightly self-edited.

I have tried to give some conscientious
thoughts to this matter of mental health services at City College, especially in view of
the unprecedented volume of communications to
this Board. I would like to share my view as
to where the matter stands at the present time.
Unfortunately, I don't think there is a solution which would be a particularly constructive one at this time. I think there are four
issues, and I think these issues are the following: *First,* is there a likelihood of dis-
continuing mental health services? *Secondly,*
what services should be undertaken for the
program? *Third,* who should have the ultimate
responsibility for the program? and *Fourth,*
a separable question, what persons should be
employed to administer the program?

On the first question of discontinuance of the
program, it is my own view that this is to a
large extent a "red herring." It has been
the basis of most of the phone calls and most
of the letters that I received; but the fact
is that nobody has urged that the program be
be discontinued. I believe that there is a
consensus that we continue with some kind of
mental health service on the campus, and I
think that in a real sense there has been a
disservice to the discussion by injecting the
prospect of the termination of any service as
an issue.

Secondly, I would think that before the Board
takes any action, someone ought to delineate
what services will be rendered. We are dealing
with a tuition-free institution, an institu-

192

tion that is very rapidly approaching the limits of its spending ability. My general feeling from talking with some of the good professionals who have called me is that the functions of a mental health service on the campus within the limits of our resources should be those of crisis intervention and of referral. Within the strictures of realistic budgeting, I cannot see that we can provide intermediate care, not to mention long-term care. But before we institute any commitment to a permanent program I think that it is incumbent on this Board to state the limit of services it intends to furnish.

The third problem is a very difficult problem and it is the problem of who accepts the ultimate responsibility for the services. This is very difficult, because when the college operates an academic program, an occupational program, or even a recreational or physical ed program, there are layers of trained administrators and other people who have a common experience in the supervision of programming and the understanding of it. The thing that bothers me about the college itself operating a mental health program is that there is no ultimate depth of professional ability to make informed judgments. I am not just concerned with that glib word "evaluation," but rather with the fact that there is not a layer of trained professionals who have a history of skill in judging the direction, the competency, and the fruitfulness of the program. I would be very happy, for example, if there were a County Mental Health establishment with which we could contract and be confident of the result, but I think the point is well made that there is a tremendous amount of criticism of that agency. There is a State Health Department report on the subject which is extremely critical of County Mental Health Services and, before I would vote for a contract with County Mental Health, I would want at least to have a much deeper knowledge of what was involved in that report.

Finally, there is the entirely separable question of what faculty members or what professionals should be employed to administer the program. I don't think we should be bound by any expression of public support which is centered on the premise that there are only two people who can run the program. We have all kinds of ways of setting up the program, and some well-defined ways of choosing personnel. Even though there is a substantial volume of support, I don't believe that personnel choices should be made on that basis. I say that without in any way being critical of the present administrative director and clinical coordinator of the MHP as to their professional capacity. The fact of the matter is that the kind of program we have and the ultimate responsibility for it are different questions from the personnel questions. A general sentiment for a continuing mental health program does not imply that any two particular persons must be appointed to the positions involved.

The place where I unhappily find myself is that after talking with many people in the mental health field it now appears that there is not a presently existing institution which can come in and take over the ultimate responsibility for a program. That is disappointing because it is my feeling that that is precisely what should happen. I cannot move away from the feeling that we lack the depth of ultimate professional responsibility that is involved in running the program ourselves. So, I have to say at this point that I think that we are going to have to continue to struggle with this problem a while longer even though the present setup is not satisfactory to the people who are working at it. I think it would be a very costly mistake to assume that this program ought permanently to be a function of the college, administered by the college itself. Distinguish that from the purchase of services, or the furnishing of services. I have read quite a bit on the division of the city into its various mental health agencies, but I do not know of one which is both willing and able to run the program. The city's mental health services are divided on a geographical basis. If any agency is not located in the particular district of the city in which the college is located, then apparently that agency cannot serve the college. I am sure there are some good agencies but they are not in a position to do the job. I would have considerable confidence, for example, if the Mt. Zion outpatient clinic would take over the program, but they say that they are not able to do so.

I am thus opposed to voting on a permanent proposal at this time, not because of a lack of sympathy for having these services on campus, but I am lost because I do not see that any one of the available choices as a long-term solution to the problem makes a great deal of sense to me. (Governor F., May, 1975)

Following Governor F.'s remarks I was given another opportunity to speak.

The Administrative Director of the MHP pointed out that the program has been closely evaluated regularly by the people who administer the program and the medical director spends a great deal of time with them on a regular bais evaluating everything they do -- they are not autonomous in any sense. He said he had asked the administration at the college many times to do an evaluation of its own on the program, but one has not been done.

Governor E. (who had not yet resigned from the Board) said he had been involved with the program at its inception and it was never at any time intended that City College would undertake this program as one of its basic programs- it was to be operated through outside agencies who were interested in the health program. Neither was it ever intended that any district or college money be used for the program. (Govvernor E. was here guilty of either lying about or forgetting his original understandings with the funding agencies of the MHP. Recall the passage quoted earlier from a letter which he authored, as President of City College, indicating his intention to "provide funds from the regular City College budget," when outside funding had expired.) Governor E. does not believe that the program should be undertaken as

195

one of the basic programs at City College and if it is going to continue, it should continue under the auspices of outside agencies and be evaluated by those agencies as the college does not possess the expertise to do so.

The Chancellor-Superintendent said that the question that has to be answered is -- what is the responsibility of the District as it relates to delivery of mental health services. This should be addressed not only to City College, but to the clientele of the entire district, including the Community College Centers. A decision will have to be made as to what commitment the district should make with its own funds, and so far no parameters have been developed. He feels that Mental Health cannot take priority over instruction, nor can it take priority over some of the other student welfare functions. He also pointed out that if a permanent staff is developed, this would be an irrevocable commitment and it is for that reason he had asked for the study of the Mental Health Program by staff and the staff had recommended that it be continued under sub-contract. He feels this is a reasonable recommendation. If this service is extended to all the Community College Centers, there would be a budget amounting to several hundred thousand dollars and he does not feel the district is ready to make this commitment. (Minutes, Board of Governors' Meeting, May, 1975)

Several of the opinions expressed by Governors E. and F. and the Chancellor-Superintendent are worth considering, primarily for their psychological consequences. Governor F., by espousing the view that "there is not a layer of trained professionals who have a history of skill in judging the direction, the competency, and the fruitfulness of the program," chose to be blind to the ongoing evaluations and consultations which characterized the five years of sponsorship..

196

of the MHP by three professional community agencies.
By whitewashing the large "layer of professionals"
who had historically worked in and with the MHP, Governor E. seemed to imply that the MHP could operate,
with impunity, without standards of competency and
effectiveness. Such an implication would certainly
conjure up great apprehensions over college adoption of
such a program.

Governor F. also made a point of mentioning that
the "good professionals" with whom he spoke had indicated that the functions of the MHP "should" be
crisis intervention and referral. Since these functions were already the clinical cornerstones of the
MHP, his comments would be totally irrelevant, unless
they could be construed to mean that the MHP was presently engaging in, or planning to offer, long-term
care to students. When he states that "I cannot see
that we can provide intermediate care, not to mention
long-term care" in relation to "realistic" budgeting,
he is arousing fears that the MHP will function like,
or duplicate, community psychiatric agencies. Such a
program would, of course, serve no legitimate purpose, nor deserve any expenditure of college funds.

Governor E., by fallaciously stating that there
was never an intention "that any district or college

money be used for the program," left the impression that the MHP was an interloper which had no entitlement to college support. He attempted to establish that the "demonstration" project was to operate indefinitely with external funding, rather than become a "basic" program of the college. By being depicted as inordinately acquisitive "outsiders," our qualifications for college support were suspect.

The Chancellor-Superintendent makes, in his comments, two emotional appeals. By alluding to the possibility of extending mental health services to the Community College Centers, he raises the spectre of a program which could have ungovernable growth and costs. Somehow the MHP would not be subject to the normative checks and balances to which other college programs were subject.

The Chancellor-Superintendent's point that he feels the (administrative) staff's recommendation to sub-contract the MHP under SFCMHS auspices is "reasonable," has comic overtones, yet is important for its psychological impact. The comicality stems from the fact that the staff made recommendations for SFCMHS sponsorship of the MHP under sub-contract, long before a "study" was consummated. Those recommendations were admittedly implementations of the

Chancellor-Superintendent's orders. Therefore, the Chancellor-Superintendent was, strictly speaking, finding his own recommendations reasonable. Yet in terms of its psychological impact, this was an important interjection, since it left the false impression that an independent administrative staff had conducted an intensive study, the findings of which it was recommending to a presumably neutral Chancellor Superintendent.

The results of the May, 1975 Board of Governors' meeting were ambiguous. Only two, "conservative," Governors and the Chancellor-Superintendent addressed the subject of the disposition of the MHP. Thus, many of the persons who attended the meeting inferred that the County Plan would assuredly be imposed upon the MHP. A few of them even offered me condolences afterward. On the other hand, the inscrutable silence of the majority of Governors, and Governor F.'s admission of being "lost" because he did not discern a "long-term solution to the problem" (of the MHP) left Ms. Quan Holden and me with optimism, however tenuous.

The Board of Governors Meeting, June 1975

Ms. Quan Holden and I were informed through the Dean of Students that the Chancellor-Superintendent would soon present a resolution to the Board of Governors which would authorize City College to enter into an agreement with the SFCMHS, to provide mental health services during the period July 1, 1975 through June 30, 1976, in the amount of $60,000.

Our strategy was to again bombard the Board of Governors with letters and phone calls from a wide variety of sources. The Bay Area graduate schools which had used the MHP as a field placement for their students sent many letters. The WCMHS and PF were also enlisted in the mail campaign. Faculty through-out City College were informed of the Chancellor-Sup-erintendent's proposed resolution and requested to support our plan for college adoption of the MHP. Our greatest investment of time and energy, however, went into our plans for the critical Board meeting itself, which we learned would take place in June, 1975.

We spoke with the Chairperson of the Personnel Committee of the Academic Senate who had already given generously of his time and assistance. He again of-fered to speak in our behalf at the Board meeting. I next called Dr. L., the Co-Director of the Mt. Zion Crisis Clinic, to request his participation as a pro-gram spokesman at the Board meeting. He readily consented; however, he and I had to first overcome an

200

inevitable shortcoming. His knowledge of the MHP --
its history, services, costs, personnel, conflicts with
the college administration, etc. -- was superficial.
He suggested that we confer in order to plan in
meticulous detail the scope and thrust of his presentation to the Board. In our conference I informed
D. L., with great specificity, of the clinical and
administrative workings of the MHP. More importantly,
I recommended exactly what points of information should
be highlighted in his presentation. On the basis of
the information we discussed, he would compose a
speech to the Board.

One additional measure which Ms. Quan Holden and
I planned was the use of a particular article which appeared recently in the *San Francisco Chronicle* (1975).
This article reported the State's scathing indictment
of the services provided by the SFCMHS. Ms. Quan
Holden and I had strong compunctions about exploiting
the hardships of another mental health agency for our
own purposes. We feared that our impolitic actions might
have untoward repercussions for the relations between
the SFCMHS and the MHP, which heretofore had been very
positive. After all, the WCMHS, one of our original
program sponsors and subsidizers, was an administrative
entity of the SFCMHS. I, therefore, called the Clini-

cal Assistant to the Program Chief of SFCMHS to inform him of our intention to use the State's criticisms of his agency in order to strengthen our case for a refutation of the County Plan. I expressed the hope that our actions would not be construed as a genuine attempt to denigrate the SFCMHS *per se*, but rather as an unfortunate expediency in our pursuit of an alternative plan for college integration of the MHP. I offered to try to rectify any damage our strategy might cause to the reputation of the SFCMHS; following, of course, the Board meeting. The Clinical Assistant was unperturbed and reassuring. He indicated a full understanding of the political dynamics which were precipitating our actions and indicated that he did not anticipate that acrimony would result from our use of the adverse newspaper publicity.

As expected, in June, 1975, the Chancellor-Superintendent submitted a resolution to the Board of Governors which authorized a contract for the SFCMHS to administer the MHP in the coming academic year.

> The Chairperson of the Personnel Committee spoke in support of continuing the program under its present status. He requested that consideration be given to incorporating the MHP as part of the overall college program (Student Health Service); also that the administrative director and clinical coordinator be hired as permanent faculty members. (Minutes, Board of Governors' Meeting, June, 1975)

Dr. L. first introduced himself as the Co-Director of the Mt. Zion Crisis Clinic and as lecturer at San Francisco State in the Graduate School of Rehabilitation Counseling. He then went on to say:

> Over the last four years I have become increasingly aware of the extremely high quality and effective service and training offered by the MHP at City College.
>
> First and foremost, the MHP provides a unique and exceptional service. There are impressive and ever-increasing figures of utilization, and I am sure that you are most familiar with those. Also essential is the fact that the services are *unique* and *convenient*. They are *on-campus* and in new quarters, more attractive and inviting than ever before. The professionals providing services are extremely skilled, generally, but even more important are exceptionally well-versed in the kinds of difficulties and stresses which often plague students. For those students engaged in *study-work programs*, as most students at the college are, with little time available outside of their scheduled activities, the convenient placement of high quality services is an essential factor in usage.
>
> The whole notion of prevention, so prominent a concept in the mental health field over the past ten years, is based in large part on increasing the likelihood that services offered will be utilized. By staffing the mental health program with skilled professionals, highly conversant with the specific difficulties usually arising for people in this kind of setting, and locating those services in a geographically convenient place, where access to them is easy, one tremendously increases the likelihood that such services will be used. In addition, contact of a preventive and educational nature with an excess of 1,000 students (per year) in the classroom is an extremely important factor in prevention. The campus MHP is almost ideal in the way it offers both crisis and preventive services.

203

One recently published study concerning the
Mental Health Services offered at junior colleges
throughout the country indicates that City College is in the forefront of colleges across the
country in providing mental health services. Such
a position is certainly an enviable one.

Another study conducted on the City College
campus has shown a *significantly lower drop-
out rate* for those students who utilize the
MHP's services as opposed to the student population as a whole.

I won't belabor figures too much, but I would
like to mention a few which I think bear on this
subject directly and indirectly:

First, the cost per unit of contact at City
College MHP ranges between $20 and $30, de-
pending on whether the preventive educational
work done in the classroom is considered. This
work is done almost totally by trained professional staff. The unit cost compares extremely
favorably with unit costs at most outpatient
clinics, where clients are usually seen by
trainees. So here at City College you have
trained professional staff doing the primary
contact and intervention, as compared with
trainees in mental health disciplines doing
most of the treatment work at the other outpatient clinics in the City.

When these costs per unit figures are compared
with some of the figures for County Outpatient
Treatment recently made public, the discrepan-
cy in costs becomes almost unbelievable -- a
couple of County Outpatient Units exceed $100.
These are largely the result of extremely top-
heavy administrative costs. In addition, if
one reads the most recent State Health Department Survey of Mental Health Services in San
Francisco, one is left with the distinct impression that the quality and effectiveness of
the services and the programs in the County is
extremely variable, at best.

Therefore, I believe that to look to the County
to try and help in this instance seems misguided.
What you currently have is an efficiently oper-

operating, high-quality service which performs evaluations, does crisis intervention and brief treatment, and makes referrals for intermediate and long-term treatment where necessary. These, it seems to me, are ideal goals for such a service. In addition to the service given by the MHP there is also a small training function for some of the very best young people to enter the ranks of the mental health profession. Rehabilitation Counseling graduate students from S.F. State and social work students in the Bay Area vie for the few places available for training in this program. The service is regarded as an outstanding placement. Not just for the kinds of problems one can see and work with, but also for the high level of supervisory competence of the staff. My colleagues at Mt. Zion's Department of Psychiatry and those from the Westside Community Mental Health Center (Dr. L. here mentions the names of five prominent clinicians and administrators) have all asked that I convey their exceptionally high regard for the services and training which are offered in the MHP. They have asked me to urge strongly that the Board vote unanimously to fully incorporate this vital service, the MHP, into the overall college program.

Let me reiterate: the service offered here is unique and highly beneficial -- there is no duplication of these services elsewhere within the City for students of City College. Failure to insure its existence and continued quality care would, in our view, constitute a deep disservice to the constituency it serves and to the citizens of the City.

Dr. L. offers the following impressions of the Board meeting:

I was struck by the position of the Chancellor-Superintendent. He seemed so rigid and backward. He wanted to cut away a program which was helping to make City College a good school. His approach was antagonistic and provocative. At one point, soon after I had finished speaking, he asked, "If you think so highly of the MHP, why don't you have your friends at Mt.

Zion and WCMHS fund it?" I told him that I had
no authority over the expenditure of such funds.
Also, I thought that the MHP was ultimately the
fiscal responsibility of the college. I thought
the Chancellor-Superintendent had an archaic,
meat-and-potatoes attitude toward students and
the provision of psychological services. He
may have thought the MHP was somewhat important,
but certainly not essential to the college.
He was probably in the mainstream of many administrators of institutions during that austere
time, seeking to conserve funds by cutting programs which might be regarded as frills. My
own interest in aiding the MHP stemmed from the
many positive things I had heard about it from
my colleagues at Mt. Zion. I had a sense that
it was a worthwhile, winnable cause. No one
else had stepped forward (at Mt. Zion), I had
the energy and enjoy a good fight, especially
one that can be won. My presentation to the
Board caused me a great deal of anxiety, but
since I believed in the MHP, it was good to
feel righteously indignant.

The following are some of the remarks which

I made to the Board in my presentation:

At our last meeting we discussed some of the
options available to the MHP. As you know, the
college administration supports the continuance
of the program at its present fiscal level,
$60,000 a year. Therefore, the only unresolved
issues are sponsorship and permanence.

One option which is being offered tonight by the
college administrative staff is to allocate the
funds to the SFCMHS in order to have it administer the MHP. Our objections to this plan are
many, but two in particular stand out. First,
the SFCMHS has been under severe and justifiable
criticism for some time from the State due to
its lack of effectiveness, creativity and cost
control. I would like to call your attention to
the newspaper article (*San Francisco Chronicle*)
which you have before you (copies of the article
were distributed to the Governors when I came
to the podium).

At this point I excerpted and read from the newspaper article the following statements:

> San Francisco's vaunted community mental health program is a mess and is need of a major overhaul.
>
> San Francisco is a "poor place" for children and youth with psychological and emotional difficulties, and services to this group are "badly fragmented and disorganized."
>
> An unresponsive civil service system and an over-reliance on traditional therapies make a bad situation even worse.
>
> According to the (State) study, "the imbalance of service may also reflect another serious deficit found during the survey: namely, that the administration and managerial structure of the mental health program at both the district and central mental health services level is inadequate to develop comprehensive, well-balanced services.

After quoting from the newspaper article, I proceeded:

> Secondly, as indicated in the SFCMHS Program Chief's letter to the ADBA (I then pointedly asked if the Board had read the letter, the contents of which had earlier been grudgingly released to us by the Acting President), the SFCMHS makes it clear that it has no commitment whatsoever to our program and that any contract it made with City College would imply no support or assistance to the program beyond one year. Essentially, then, the County Plan would transfer responsibility for the operation of the program from those of us who have provided excellent services on this campus for over five years to an absentee sponsoring agency which has no experience with our students on this campus and which, as the State report indicates, provides services to youth which are "badly disorganized."

One additional facet of the County Plan is important. In over five years the SFCMHS has never indicated even a slight interest or initiative with respect to the MHP. It has repeatedly, over the years, turned down our requests for funding and clinical manpower. Even in this present situation it has shown no initiative, other than to respond to a request that it receive $60,000 in return for its sponsorship. By its own admission, its commitment to the MHP is nonexistent. Furthermore, the Board should note that a decision to have the SFCMHS adopt the MHP would, in effect, mean that the Board of Governors will be abdicating its authority to the County Board of Supervisors with respect to who administers and staffs the MHP (I had gleaned this particular political insight from the SFCMHS Clinical Assistant. It was employed to create doubts in the minds of the Governors about the extent of their future authority over the MHP.) I think the implications of that transfer of authority are obvious (I did not really fathom the implications myself, but it seemed that a vague, ominous remark of that sort would further aggravate doubts about the County Plan.) Clearly, the County Plan would be a huge step backward for City College which will serve to destroy the MHP.

As indicated in our last meeting, we seek a resolution from the Board of Governors to adopt the MHP by hiring Ms. Quan Holden and me. The MHP continues to gain prominence throughout the state and nation. Ms. Quan Holden and I will be serving on the Chancellor of Community Colleges' Ad Hoc Committee to recommend legislation related to campus mental health services in California. This past month I have been interviewed for television coverage of our program. As we continue to gain prominence and respect, we find ourselves in an increasingly contradictory and embarrassing position. We are looked to for long-range leadership in this field. Yet on our own campus we have not yet been accorded the long-range security with which to carry out our far-reaching programs on this campus or elsewhere in the state.

208

Following my presentation, Ms. Quan Holden made
a brief but telling statement which emphasized our
dedication to the MHP and our entitlement to parity
with other college personnel. It was then the college administration's turn to advocate its resolution.

> The Acting President spoke to the resolution,
> noting there are two issues involved: (1) the
> propriety of an educational institution sup-
> plying this type of service and (2) the fact
> that there is a county agency more prepared to
> handle this function. He said that the SFCMHS,
> under the agreement, would assume the responsi-
> bility of providing mental health services at
> the college and would supplement the present
> staff with some of their own staff members.
> (At this juncture Governor C. jocularly blurted
> out that he had never known the county to
> give such assistance before.) SFCMHS would
> sub-contract with the Progress Foundation
> (which had not officially agreed to do so),
> but would be accountable to City College. It
> is understood that the present Administrative
> Director and Clinical Coordinator would remain
> with the program as Progress Foundation employees.

At this point, as we had planned and hoped, one
of the Governors requested the ADBA to read the letter
of agreement from the SFCMHS Program Chief. Following
the reading of the letter, Governor F. took the initiative.

> Governor F. said he was not willing to vote on
> turning the MHP over to the SFCMHS until the
> Board is apprised of the extent of the contract
> to be entered into. He feels the points out-
> lined justify the continuance of the program
> and as money is already budgeted, there is no
> time pressure because of budget requirements;
> however, the uncertainties that lie behind the
> resolution in its present form preclude adop-

tion as written. Governor F. believes the program should be continued in its present status for an additional year and during that period of time the question of who would provide mental health services on campus can be investigated and a permanent solution sought. Governor F. pointed out that the question of the people to be hired is entirely a separable question from that of policy and responsibility for the program.

Governor D. said he concurred with Governor F., that a basic mental health program should be continued for the coming year as the money has been budgeted. He suggested that all facets of the program be examined during the coming year and a decision made as to continuance of the program on a permanent basis.

The Chancellor-Superintendent said that his concern relates to the priority of this program. He noted that when the college entered into the agreement to supply mental health services, it was at the behest of community groups who picked up the full cost. Since that time the college has put money into the program, but it was never the intention to take over this responsibility which primarily belongs to the county. He feels that if a permanent commitment is made by the college, it would mean committing local funds. If funds such as these are transferred to this program, it would mean establishment of a priority and service which in actuality should be available to every adult in San Francisco because every adult in San Francisco is a potential student. If the service is available at City College, then it should also be available at all the Community College Centers. The Chancellor-Superintendent feels that the district should not move into mental health care on a permanent basis, but should continue to serve at the college, as in the past, until a permanent solution is found. He said he would be willing to withdraw the resolution, keep the budgeted amount, and see if satisfactory negotiations can be concluded with the SFCMHS to continue with the Progress Foundation at the present level. He does not feel that permanent staffing is the answer to the problem. He noted

210

that Dr. O. (the incoming President) has considerable training in counseling and educational
psychology and it is his hope that when he arrives on campus he might establish parameters
for this service. He withdrew his resolution.
(Minutes, Board of Governors Meeting, June,
1975)

Not included in the Board minutes was the Chancellor-Superintendent's peroration, "I have
great respect for Mr. Amada's professional
skills, but have no respect for the way in which
he has politicized this matter." He did not
elaborate on the point, and no Governor ver-
bally responded to it. (Ms. Quan Holden)

The following impressions of the Board meeting

are noteworthy:

I think that the County Plan was strictly a
personal creation of one man, the Chancellor-
Superintendent. He preferred to regard the MHP
as a bandaid service to students. His attitudes
seem to lack a social philosophy. When he gets
his mind on something, there is no logic to it.
Two sides of an argument become irrelevant
philosophically. I believe the budgetary concerns he expressed were a "red herring." He
personalized the conflict and his anger toward
you in particular caused him to go at things
with a vengeance. The Board, at that time,
were reticent to disagree with him because he
had suffered a recent loss over the hiring of
President O. The administrators who were involved (the ADBA and the Dean of Students) did
not examine the rights and wrongs of the situation; they were going to carry out the
Chancellor-Superintendent's orders "to the
death." I think the Chancellor-Superintendent's
ostensible financial concerns were used to
camouflage his primary wish: to get rid of
you. In addition, your program was non-trad-
itional and, therefore, viewed by such trad-
itionalists as the Chancellor-Superintendent,
as deviant and subversive. As for myself, as
a minority person, I felt strongly supportive
of the MHP, which seemed to have all the right

211

ingredients. I was beginning to feel burned out by my own participation in the chronic struggle which was going on, but it was a cause worth fighting for. For a time it seemed to be a matter of which side would have the energy to endure. Unlike a lot of such conflicts, however, this one ultimately had a satisfactory, almost storybook ending. (Chairperson, Personnel Committee, Academic Senate)

In the later summer, 1975, the Board of Governors perfunctorily ratified a resolution to contract with Progress Foundation to provide mental health services during the period of September 1, 1975 through June 30, 1976, in the amount of $60,000. The MHP had won a reprieve; another year in which to plan and quest for permanency.

A Meeting with the Chancellor-Superintendent

Early in the Fall semester, 1975, Ms. Quan Holden and I requested a meeting with the Chancellor-Superintendent. We hoped that the call for a meeting would be construed as a gesture of goodwill which might assuage some of the Chancellor-Superintendent's resentment over our recent counterplotting. In attendance were the Chancellor-Superintendent, the ADBA (who had recently been promoted to the position of Assistant to the Chancellor-Superintendent), the Dean of Students, the Coordinator of Student Health Services, Ms. Quan Holden and I.

You began the meeting by commenting that we
hoped to heal some of the wounds which our recent conflict wrought. You stated our regret-
ting the necessity for confrontation with the
college administration and our wish to now seek
avenues for reconciliation with them. When you
concluded your comments, the Chancellor-Superintendent angrily accused you of bypassing him
from the start and using militant methods of
achieving ends which were achievable by more
conventional means. You reminded him of your
conference of about one year ago, in which he
suggested that you resign yourself to the County Plan. You remarked that he was fully consulted, at the outset, of our objectives, and
chose to oppose them.

The discussion took a more personal turn when
the Chancellor-Superintendent made innuendoes
about your private psychotherapy practice. He
implied that there was something insidious
about your working at the college four days
and maintaining a private practice one day. You
replied that that arrangement had existed for
many years and was always deemed acceptable by
the contracting agencies. It had never been
considered questionable. You added that you
would prefer to increase your time at the college, but the impermanence of the program made
it necessary to maintain an active private practice as a hedge against losing your college job.

The Chancellor-Superintendent then began to prod
you by stating that despite all your efforts at
lobbying, you "lost" in the recent struggle over
the MHP. He insisted, "Why don't you admit it,
you lost, didn't you?" I thought that statement quixotic, since we had won at least a par-
tial, but significant victory during the last
several months. You "ate humble pie" by saying,
"Yes, I had lost." That reply was evidently
too matter-of-fact and unremorseful for him.
He countered, "No, don't admit that to me, admit it to yourself. You're a psychologist (an
inaccurate disciplinary designation at the time),
you know the importance of admitting such things
to oneself." You light-heartedly replied, "All
right, I'll admit it to myself." Apparently
that was not quite penitent enough, because he

213

persisted, "No, don't do that for my sake, do it
for yourself. It will make you feel better."
At that point he must have felt he had had his
"pound of flesh" since he suddenly laughed good-
naturedly and the rest of the conferees, who
until then had sat silently watching, also broke
into laughter.

At this point, the conference became more busi-
ness-like and task-oriented. The Chancellor-
Superintendent acknowledged that we were understandably under great pressure to preserve our
jobs and the MHP. He then suggested that there
would be no consideration of adding new positions beyond those already projected for the
various academic and service programs. However,
he thought a resolution of our situation might
be effected if certain other departments of the
college released their newly budgeted positions
to the MHP. Admittedly, this was a "long-shot,"
but we were advised to explore the possibilities
with the Chairpersons and Coordinators of three
departments: Student Health Services (which was
budgeted for one new nursing position), the
Counseling Department (which was slated for
two new positions), and Health Education (which
was hiring one new instructor).
    (Ms. Quan Holden)

The advice of the Chancellor-Superintendent

seemed a perfect formula for internecine warfare be-

tween the MHP and those departments which were to be

solicited for newly budgeted positions. Nevertheless,

at the time we had no recourse other than to inves-

tigate the potentialities of his advice.

In a meeting with the staff and Chairperson of

the Health Education Department, we learned that their

new instructorship position was essential to the highly

coveted expansion of that program. That department,

214

therefore, sympathetically but adamantly denied our application for its budgeted position.

We next turned to the Counseling Department. We were told that its two openings were vital to its services. Forfeiture of its projected positions would proportionately increase the already bloated student caseloads of its counseling staff. If we wished (and we did not), we could apply for the two positions ourselves, but our assignments would conform strictly to those of other counseling staff.

Reluctantly, and desperately, we next foraged the Student Health Service for a MHP position. This was fated to be a highly sensitive and explosive incursion. A nurse who had served on a temporary basis in the SHS during the academic year 1974-75 was overtly aspiring for the single projected position. When Ms. Quan Holden and I informed her and the SHS Coordinator that we would vie for that position, both naturally took umbrage with us. We were advised to look elsewhere for positions. Since the nurse had worked in the SHS only one year and our combined SHS experience totalled about ten years, we considered ourselves morally and professionally entitled to compete for the position allotted the SHS. We expressed our regrets over harboring such intentions and vowed to continue our search for better alternatives. We indicated our wish not to meddle with the new position for SHS, if at all possible. As expected, the Chancellor-Superintendent's scheme, to have us wrest a projected position from the SHS, resulted in an irreparable deterioration in the relations between the nursing and MHP staffs. I will elaborate on that point later in this chapter.

After being debarred from the positions in the Health Education and Counseling Departments, and producing an intramural furor over seeking the SHS position, it seemed advisable to discuss our findings with the Chancellor-Superintendent. I called him on the phone, explained the disappointing results of his suggestion and requested that we meet again to negotiate a resolution of the problem. He brusquely stated the following:

> You and I have nothing to discuss or negotiate. I don't negotiate these matters with (rank-and-file) staff. Look, I don't mean to be hard-nosed, but there comes a time when you must face the facts. The MHP is going to terminate at the end of this year. It is regrettable, but you'd better reconcile yourself to the reality of the situation; there are no jobs here for you.

Meetings with the President of City College

Ms. Quan Holden and I resolved to take our appeal to President O., with whom we had not yet con-

216

ferred. He and I discussed the status and prospects of the MHP in a bilateral conference. His perspective initially was that the Chancellor-Superintendent was determined not to incorporate the MHP into the college and that the outlook for the program was bleak insofar as our objectives were concerned. He gave no hint of a willingness to arrogate to himself any authority over the future pursuits of the MHP. I felt demoralized and angry with him for assuming such an administrative posture. I thought he should have allowed me to more completely review and evaluate the administrative problems of the MHP. I believed, without definite proof, that he was forejudging me and the MHP, based upon suspicions that were implanted by the Chancellor-Superintendent. My frustration with President O.'s stance caused me to disgustedly remark that I had been forced to fight his predecessor and if he, too, chose to ally himself with the Chancellor-Superintendent, I would, very reluctantly, oppose him with every resource at my command. He serenely stated that he knew of my prior lobbying activities, regretted the conflictual state of affairs and, in a non-censorious manner, indicated that I was free to exercise whatever prerogatives I felt were necessary to defend the MHP.

217

Following my meeting with President O., Ms. Quan Holden and I experienced a three week period of demoralization and immobilization. We felt that the MHP was doomed to extinction; that our community and campus allies had been depleted by our chronic struggles and that we were too psychologically enervated and politically impotent to mount yet another campaign to beat an antagonistic college administration. Our last thread of hope, to win President O. as an advocate of the MHP, seemed misguided and peurile.

Ms. Quan Holden then had a "revelation" which, in retrospect, was a watershed moment in the history of the MHP. She reasoned that President O. was unfavorable to me, at least partially, because of the opprobrium attached to my reputation with the college administration. Also, perhaps being a woman and a minority member (having Black and Asian ancestry), she could develop rapport with President O. more readily than I.

> I went to see President O. on a Friday when he seemed to be winding down. He was friendly and attentive. I reviewed the history of the MHP and provided our perspective of the disputes with the Chancellor-Superintendent. He was warm and inquired about my accent (Trinidadian) and ethnic background. I then explained to him that, from our standpoint, you had been maligned by the college administration because you did what was necessary to prevent them from decimating the program. Because you were male and

consistently the more visible of the two of us
as Director of the Program, you were charged
with being disruptive and a malcontent.

Something positive occurred in this meeting.
We knew the President was dissatisfied with
the direction and scope of the Counseling Department. He regarded their services to be
academic "advisement," rather than intensive
counseling. I raised the possibility of our
being in a position to assist him in the in-
novations of such service programs at the college. He was receptive, saying he'd think
about it. (Ms. Quan Holden)

Ms. Quan Holden and I subsequently met with

President O., who was somewhat reassuring. We asked

if there were ways in which we could assist him in

smoothing the way for college adoption of the MHP.

He advised us not to interfere in his handling of

the matter. He would soon be canvassing his admin-

istrative staff to assess their amenability to the

permanent integration of the MHP. With a great deal

of relief, Ms. Quan Holden and I determined that we

would totally refrain from lobbying activities. We

resolved to place implicit confidence and trust in

President O.

President O. soon informed us that he would

be discussing the matter of establishing two per-

manent MHP positions with the Chancellor-Superintend-

ent. The earliest reports from him indicated that the

Chancellor-Superintendent, with many reservations,

was willing to assume a *laissez-faire* attitude toward the President's interest in permanent MHP positions. Apparently he would not block a conscientious attempt by President O. to adopt the MHP. A brief period ensued during which we received reports from the Dean of Students that the Chancellor-Superintendent was reappraising and perhaps reversing his decision to allow President O. to recommend MHP permanency. Finally, we learned that the President would, unimpeded by the Chancellor-Superintendent, recommend college adoption of the two MHP positions to the Board of Governors.

Why did President O. swing over to supporting the permanency of the MHP? We were not privy to his inner thoughts or to his discussions with the Chancellor-Superintendent. Therefore, the following explanations are speculative. First, he may have realized that the Chancellor-Superintendent's opposition to program permanency was largely a personal aversion to me. If he himself did not have such feelings about Ms. Quan Holden and me, that may have given him cause to reflect skeptically on the Chancellor-Superintendent's overall recommendations. Secondly, the rapport which he initially established with Ms. Quan Holden, and later with me, may have, in itself, been an important intangible factor in his supporting our request for help. Finally, President O. was a relative newcomer to the City College campus. He very likely wished to demonstrate early in his incumbency his administrative independence. One means of achieving administrative autonomy would be through programmatic and philosophical transformations of the campus. The MHP may have been one of the first authentic tests of his administrative independence and fortitude. If he himself regarded it as such, that may account, in part, for why he decided to shoulder the unsavory responsibility of advocating its permanence.

The Board of Governors' Meeting

Throughout our strivings for program permanency, Ms. Quan Holden and I were acutely aware of a perilous pitfall to that plan. Since the permanent integration of the MHP would constitute the adoption of two "new" positions in the college district, the procedure for hiring MHP staff would, by law, require an open and competitive application process. Therefore, despite our combined eleven years of experience in the MHP, Ms. Quan Holden and I were vulnerable to displacement by job aspirants who had never served in the program. I will return to the subject of the hiring procedures later in this chapter.

Upon President O.'s recommendation, a resolution was placed before the Board of Governors to establish two full-time faculty-status positions in the
MHP. This resolution did not determine which particular personnel would staff the MHP. It authorized
only the adoption of program positions. The separate
matter of hiring specific individuals to staff the MHP
would be encompassed in another resolution at a subsequent Board meeting.

The Board of Governors met in closed Executive
Session prior to the public Board meeting. They con-
vened the public meeting almost two hours later than
its scheduled starting time. While anxiously awaiting the Board's arrival, Ms. Quan Holden and I alter-
nately considered and dismissed the possibility that
this protracted delay was due to a Board debate over
the MHP. There were many other items on the agenda,
but, unfortunately, none so controversial as the MHP.

The following is a summarization of the Executive Session:

> The Executive Session was largely taken up
> with a discussion of the pro's and con's of
> hiring you. There was strong resistance to
> you as a person. You were considered abrasive.
> You had gone outside channels and some impor-
> tant people didn't like that. Let's face it,
> you were the one who spearheaded the program.
> So, you naturally were blamed and disliked for
> how you fought for it. Don't take it per-

222

sonally. It could have been anyone, even me, and the reaction would have been the same. I felt that some people were confusing you with the program. I spoke in your behalf. I thought it was a good, important program. I said that if, in time, we don't like the guy (me), we can get rid of him later, but the fact is, the MHP has merit. You did get good support from some other Board members.

Some of the objections raised had to do with the heavy costs of tenuring two more positions. There was also mention made of the fact that you had maintained a private psychotherapy practice off-campus and that, therefore, you didn't really need the MHP position. Perhaps your commitment to the MHP was negligible due to your other professional work. Also, I won't say who they were, but you had some key people from the administrative staff in there who were really opposed to you (the Dean of Students and the Assistant to the Chancellor-Superintendent were, I believe, the only administrative staff in attendance at the Executive Session.) But the consensus was that the MHP was a good and necessary service. The arguments against your personality, that you were a pain in the ass, were not a good reason for rejecting the whole package. You were persistent and had important friends, so you won out.
     (Governor B.)

Apparently, during the discussion in the Executive Session two separate, but interrelated, issues were merged: my suitability for college employment, and the permanent adoption of the MHP. Although the current resolution authorized only program adoption, my opponents were not naive. They fully realized that my commitment to the MHP was far from "negligible," and that I would compete ferociously for one of the two permanent positions. They also realized that once

223

the decisive step of authorizing permanent program positions was taken, my professional qualifications for
one of the assignments would be extremely difficult to
repudiate. Therefore, it was their sophistication,
not their confusion, which caused my adversaries to
merge the question of program permanence with the matter of my professional and personal qualifications.

In the public Board meeting the resolution for
authorizing the college adoption of two MHP positions
was uneventfully passed.

Hiring Procedures

The Dean of Students appointed the Coordinator
of SHS to serve as Chairperson of the Hiring Committee
assigned to interview and evaluate MHP job applicants.
He directed her to recruit to the committee a representative cross-section of college personnel. If possible,
she was to organize a committee whose membership had
an ethnic, disciplinary and female-male balance.

Although we acknowledged the legal requirements
which mandated a competitive hiring procedure, Ms. Quan
Holden and I felt humiliated and indignant over having
to apply for jobs which materialized largely due to
our own efforts. Our humiliation was compounded when
the Dean requested that Ms. Quan Holden and I write up

our job descriptions in order to assist the college
administration in accurately advertising the prospective MHP positions statewide.

At about this time, the Dean of Students selected the SHS Coordinator to also serve as Chairperson of
the Hiring Committee assigned to interview applicants
for the prospective nursing position. In an attempt
to make amends for seeking to appropriate that position
for ourselves, Ms. Quan Holden and I individually
sought out the nurse, Ms. U., who had been actively
aspiring to qualify for that job. We conveyed our
support of her candidacy for the permanent nursing position. A short time afterward I was invited by the
SHS Coordinator to serve on the Hiring Committee for
for the nursing position. Also serving on that committee were a SHS secretary, the SHS office manager,
and one SHS nurse. Its Chairperson, as indicated
earlier, was the SHS Coordinator.

My impression was that the Hiring Committee was
flagrantly non-representative and that the hiring of
Ms. U. was a foregone conclusion. The SHS Coordinator
had not only publicly voiced her support of Ms. U.;
she had even written a letter of recommendation for
her to the Hiring Committee of which she was Chairperson! In my estimation, her respective roles as

SHS Coordinator and Chairperson of the Hiring Committee for SHS positions constituted a scandalous conflict of interest. Each member of the Hiring Committee, including me, was an organizational subordinate of the SHS Coordinator. Each was undoubtedly alive to the fact that the SHS Coordinator would brook little opposition to the hiring of Ms. U.

After a period of reviewing the applicants' resumes and applications, the Hiring Committee interviewed in person about seven or eight nurses. It then selected two finalists who were recommended to President O. for his final determination: Ms. U. and another nurse of comparable professional experience. I had two distinct impressions of this process. First, of all the interviewees, Ms. U. was the most unnerved and inarticulate in the interviewing situation. In response, the committee was extremely solicitous and eager to comfort her. Her interview was at least ten minutes shorter than those of the other applicants. Second, in my view, the other finalist selected by the committee, as compared with those other applicants who were interviewed, was Ms. U.'s weakest professional competitor. Her professional experience and sophistication seemed to me to be inferior to several of the other nurses

226

who were interviewed. Interestingly, one of the interviewees, after discovering the membership of the Hiring Committee and the fact that Ms. U. had already been a temporary employee of the SHS for one year and was now applying for permanent employment, became enraged, stated that she regarded her interview as pointless and left the room in a huff. A few days later, President O. interviewed the two nurse finalists in the morning and selected Ms. U. in the afternoon.

Why did I passively support the selection of Ms. U., since I considered the hiring process to be a sham and her interview unimpressive? Partly out of self-interest. I knew that the SHS Coordinator was due to be Chairperson of the Hiring Committee for the prospective MHP positions. I anticipated that any expression of doubt on my part regarding Ms. U.'s employability would result in reprisals against Ms. Quan Holden and me when the next Hiring Committee evaluated our applications for permanent employment. Secondly, despite her poor showing in the interview and my own nascent dislike for Ms. U. (based partly on the relative ease and brevity with which she was hired), I genuinely considered her to be a well qualified nurse. I thought she was entitled to permanent employment based upon her previous year of conscientious and effective professional service.

The SHS Coordinator asked me to recommend candidates for membership to the MHP Hiring Committee. I replied that, in over six and one-half years on the campus, Ms. Quan Holden and I had engendered a wide range of attitudes among the staff of the college, from extremely positive to very antagonistic. However, since my opinion was being solicited, I would naturally prefer to recommend known sympathizers. Therefore, I submitted the names of the SHS office manager, the SHS secretary (both of whom had just finished serving on the Hiring Committee for the nursing position), a City College student who worked in the SHS (students were eligible for committee membership), a psychology instructor, and the City College Enabler. This last person (an Asian-Latin American) was a former trainee in the MHP and an enthusiastic supporter of Ms. Quan Holden and me.

The SHS Coordinator aroused my suspicions immediately. My preferences for the SHS office manager and SHS secretary were completely ignored. The student I recommended was debunked on the basis of her supposed unfamiliarity with the workings of the MHP. Initially, the psychology instructor was not disentitled to committee membership, but I thought it

228

strange that the SHS Coordinator suggested that we consider, instead, an off-campus psychotherapist who had done no professional work with the MHP in over three years. The Enabler was the only recommendation which the SHS Coordinator ultimately considered acceptable.

Following my meeting with the SHS Coordinator she requested a conference with Ms. Quan Holden.

> The SHS Coordinator told me that there were "reservations" about permanently hiring you. I asked who held such reservations. She mentioned the Chancellor-Superintendent and the Dean of Students. She requested that I treat our communication as confidential. I felt caught and unfortunately consented. She then added that she also shared these reservations. After that talk I immediately spoke with you about her comments. I then returned to her and admitted that I had made a mistake in agreeing to keep our conference confidential. I advised her to consult with you immediately. (Ms. Quan Holden)

The SHS Coordinator did not consult with me, so shortly before closing time I went to see her. I told her I had heard of vague "reservations" about me and wished to know what they were and whether they might impinge upon her role as Chairperson of a committee which was considering my suitability for employment. She refused to discuss the matter then, explaining that it was closing time. She preferred to take it up the next day.

We met the next day. The SHS Coordinator stated that her reservations about me dated back several months. She cited an instance when we had attended a police science class together. She claimed that a student had asked me for advice in handling psychiatric emergencies and I had been abrupt and uninformative with him. I was dumbfounded. I queried:

> Do you mean that after six and one-half years of service, you have reservations about my employment based upon a single incident I can't even remember? For all I know, you may be absolutely correct about that incident. Even if I conceded that you are accurate (and I don't), is that supposed mishap going to outweigh my achievements in the MHP?

The SHS Coordinator said that, in her mind, it was a very important incident and that I was treating it too lightly. I told her that I refused to believe that one classroom incident was the crux of her reservations. I wanted a more credible explanation. She then stated that that was one of my problems. Whenever my work was criticized, I became defensive and unreasonable. This made it impossible to hold a rational conversation with me. I told her that I thought the incident was being brandished to camouflage feelings of resentment and vindictiveness over other, more central issues (such as our recent threat to the prospective nursing position). I also thought

230

she was employing herself as the college administration's hatchet woman by trying to mar the reputation of my professional work in order to destroy my chances to qualify for permanent employment. She obviously disagreed.

I then proceeded to question the SHS Coordinator's credibility as Chairperson of the Hiring Committee. I suggested that, rather than having an "inside track" on one of the MHP positions due to many years of dedicated and effective service, I had perhaps "two strikes" against me because of her authoritative position on the Hiring Committee. She stated that she could maintain a fairness and impartiality toward me despite her reservations and that my eligibility for permanent employment would not be jeopardized by her assignment with the committee. By this time I was feeling unquenchable rage. I told her that I had no confidence in her avowals of impartiality. My *coup de grace* was to add the following:

> If you dare to fuck with my job and my life by displaying any sign of unprofessional or unethical conduct in chairing the Hiring Committee, I will haul your ass into court. And I don't mean City College. I will sue *you*. You had better believe it.

She said that based upon knowing me, she did believe it. That ended the substantive part of our conference.

Ms. Quan Holden and I felt consternation over
the SHS Coordinator's authority over the Hiring Committee. We quickly called a meeting with the Dean
of Students to voice our concerns.

> The Dean and the SHS Coordinator were clearly
> colluding to cover up their true intentions;
> namely, to get rid of you. Consequently, by
> a feat of convoluted logic, he suggested that
> she had every right to state her reservations
> about you in confidence to me. He then accused
> me of wrong-doing by breaking that confidence.
> Even more astonishing was her version of our
> "confidential" talk. She stated that I was
> the one who had initiated the conference with
> her to discuss reservations about you. This
> was a bald lie and I said so. The Dean so
> one-sidedly supported her that it made the
> meeting meaningless. (Ms. Quan Holden)

The Hiring Committee was duly recruited, organized and scheduled by the SHS Coordinator. Serving
on the committee were two SHS nurses (one of whom is
Asian, the other White), a Black EOP counselor (who
had never had direct dealings with the MHP), an
Asian, Health Education instructor, the SHS Coordinator (who is a White nurse), and the Enabler, who stated:

> I was invited by the SHS Coordinator to serve
> on the Hiring Committee. I gladly accepted for
> two reasons: (1) I had heard about and was in-
> terested in the politics of that area (SHS) of
> the campus. I wanted to see the hassles for
> myself.

The committee received over 100 written appli-

232

cations and resumes. I didn't read them myself. Presumably, the three nurses made all
the decisions relative to which applicants
would receive personal interviews. Eventually, the number was shaved to 15-20 applicants
who were interviewed. I was surprised as to
how fine some people looked on paper and how
poorly they performed in person.

The Health Education instructor invited himself onto the committee, I believe, in order
to push for a friend, an Asian social worker
who had applied for a MHP position. The procedures and questions used for interviewing
applicants were standardized and there was a
serious air to the proceedings. Nevertheless,
I had the distinct impression that, in reality, they were searching for someone to replace
you.

Eventually, six finalists were to be selected
by the committee. A discussion took place
during which you and Ms. Quan Holden were
compared professionally with each other, as
if only one of you would be selected. The
committee felt that you were not charged up
enough during your interview and that you
came across as rather hostile. I thought so
too. (I certainly felt hostile and probably
by straining to suppress my fury and contempt,
I appeared overly casual.)

When the committee made its final determinations, you were, at first, excluded. I, alone,
had recommended you. The Health Education instructor managed to have his friend included
as a finalist. They (the committee) liked Ms.
Quan Holden and she was unanimously chosen.
Four others were then considered, not including you. At that point the EOP counselor said
that, considering your long-time service in
the MHP, it might be a "political" mistake not
to select you. After this remark, the SHS
Coordinator, without prompting from the committee to do so, wrote your name down, called
for a vote, and thereby, the group agreed to
recommend you. Thus, Ms. Quan Holden, you
and four others were to be interviewed and
evaluated by President O. for two MHP positions.

My impression of the Hiring Committee was that it was heavily biased and non-representative. It had no students, one-half of its membership was SHS nursing staff and there was prejudice against hiring you. I was shocked and disappointed by the extent of hostility there was for you on that committee.

A few days after the Hiring Committee selected its finalists and disbanded, Ms. Quan Holden and I were interviewed by President O., who presided over an administrative committee made up of the Dean of Students, the SHS Coordinator, the Dean of Business Affairs (the former Acting President) and the Coordinator of Student Welfare. Ms. Quan Holden and I considered these interviews to be straightforward and fair. President O. and his administrative committee were non-committal about our prospects and indicated only that we would be informed of their decision in a few days.

Following my interview with the President's committee, the Dean of Students called me. He suggested that my interview with the committee had been self-defeating. He faulted, in particular, my (alleged) tendency, during the interview, to avoid eye contact with the committee members. I regarded this criticism as a crass attempt to intimidate and thwart me. I had felt reasonably comfortable during my interview and vividly remembered maintaining an appropriate degree of eye contact with committee members. No other member of the committee, then or afterward, made such an extraneous allusion to my behavior during the interview. I assumed that, out of sheer desperation, the Dean was attempting to manufacture some reason, however flimsy, to submit a recommendation against hiring me.

Ms. Quan Holden and I awaited President O.'s final determinations for several, harrowing days. I then went to City College on other business. I had heard that the Dean of Students would be away, so I stopped in to ask the Dean of Business Affairs whether a decision had been reached. He lightly remarked that, yes, Ms. Quan Holden and I were selected by President O. for the two MHP positions. The decision had been reached the previous afternoon and no one had bothered to call us! I learned that the Dean of Students was in his office, so I went directly there in search of confirmation of the news.

Happily excited, I asked him if it was true, that we had been selected. He angrily wanted to know how I had found out. I mentioned that the Dean of Business Affairs had just told me. He then proceeded to tongue-lash me. He said that I was up to my old tricks again. I didn't see him about the matter, but as usual was making "end-runs" (a football term which the Dean, as a former athletic coach, was fond of using in

reference to our lobbying activities with the Board of
Governors). I reminded him of the fact that he himself had told me that he would not be in his office
that day. I had to find out what happened from some-
body, and the Dean of Business Affairs was a likely
source of such information.

The Dean then menacingly stated that he wanted
to immediately set down certain rules regarding my
future professional conduct. He would no longer tolerate the carefree and rebellious manner in which I
circumvented administrative authority. In scolding
tones he said that now that I was becoming a City
College employee, I would not be able to "get away"
with the independence and freedom which I had as a
staff member of Progress Foundation. He added that
I was a temporary employee, on probation, and that if
I resorted to any of the extremist tactics I had
used in previous years, they would be grounds for
immediate dismissal.

He next asked if I had informed Ms. Quan Holden
of the President's decision. I replied that I hadn't
had time to do that since I had heard the news only
moments before. He then said that I was under strict
orders not to tell her. It was the sole responsibility of the SHS Coordinator to inform Ms. Quan Hol-

den of the President's decision.

When I left the Dean's office, I was non-plussed. I had not exactly expected to receive his warm congratulations, but neither did I anticipate an upbraiding. I disregarded his "strict orders" and called Ms. Quan Holden to tell her the welcome news. (The SHS Coordinator, who did not know of my call to Ms. Quan Holden, never tried to reach her about the President's decision, as the Dean had suggested was her responsibility.)

I then went to the SHS facility where I told several of the staff, including the office manager, of our acceptance. The office manager, not knowing that I had already spoken with Ms. Quan Holden, called her in order to notify and congratulate her himself. The next day I called the Dean regarding a scheduling matter. He quickly commented that he had learned that the SHS office manager had called Ms. Quan Holden with the news of our appointments. He launched a tirade against me for being irresponsible and having a loose tongue. I told him that it hardly seemed necessary or conceivable to have to keep such exciting news a total secret. He responded by stating that I was already disobeying administrative orders.

The Dean's punitive treatment of me is ex-

plicable when one considers his actions in the context of the larger struggle which raged between
the college administration and the MHP. He was clearly under regular and intense pressure from the Chancellor-Superintendent to obstruct my ascendancy to a permanent college position. He demonstrably failed to
prosecute his calling. Very possibly, he was blamed
by the Chancellor-Superintendent for allowing me to
gain a permanent foothold in the college. At the
very least, he must have felt a degree of self-ad-
monishment and shame over his abortive pursuits. I
believe these factors, in addition to his personal
antipathy for me, accounted for the angry and sadis-
tic outbursts which immediately followed my appointment.

A Second Board of Governors' Meeting

In August, 1976, a resolution was placed on
the Board of Governors' agenda calling for the ratification of the presidential appointments of Ms.
Quan Holden and me as full-time SHS staff, with full
faculty status. The resolution to hire Ms. Quan
Holden and me was included in a long array of resolutions relating to many programs and departments. Such
agenda groupings were customarily ratified en masse.

238

Ms. Quan Holden and I, who were not invited to attend or speak at this meeting, were there only to witness the ratification of the MHP resolution. The set of resolutions was routinely submitted for adoption. Suddenly, Governor G. stated that he wished to call attention to agenda item number 18. To our amazement, he was referring to the MHP resolution. He wished to have an administrative representative explain what procedures had been followed in selecting Ms. Quan Holden and me. He emphasized that he was not implying doubts about our qualifications for the positions, but since we had served in the program for many years, he wanted assurances that the hiring procedures were competitive and equitable.

A call went out for an administrative spokesperson. The President, Dean of Students, the Dean of Business Affairs, the Coordinator of Student Welfare and the SHS Coordinator were all inexplicably absent. The only person in attendance, other than ourselves, who knew precisely what hiring procedures had been followed was the Chancellor-Superintendent. He maintained a stony silence while a search went on for an explanation of procedures.

Ms. Quan Holden and I felt increasing panic as the Board began to discuss postponing a decision until the September Board meeting (well after MHP services were due to recommence). A dean of instruction who was sitting behind us urged me to disregard my concerns about the propriety of speaking up. I raised my hand to the Chancellor-Superintendent who was looking straight at me. He ignored it. Finally, Governor G. descried my brisk semaphores and cordially invited Ms. Quan Holden and me to come up to the podium. We briefly explained what hiring procedures had been followed. The Board did not cavil with us over our version of the process. We were congratulated and soon thereafter the Board unanimously ratified the MHP resolution. At that decisive moment the MHP had completed its evolution from an embryonic "demonstration" project to a permanent component of the Community College District.

VI

THE AUTHORITARIAN PERSONALITY AND THE AUTHORITARIAN ORGANIZATION: THEORETICAL CONSIDERATIONS

The Mental Health Program, in its quest for permanency, encountered, first, wariness and, later, open resistance from the Chancellor-Superintendent. The Chancellor-Superintendent, as the highest administrative official of the Community College District, defined and shaped the administrative perspective of the college toward the MHP. He was also principally responsible for charting and orchestrating the administrative approaches which were used to cope with the aspirations of the program staff. In his role as the highest administrative official of the college, either directly or through organizational intermediaries, the Chancellor-Superintendent manifested a set of psychological attitudes and a mode of administrative leadership which, I believe, are universal hallmarks of the authoritarian personality and authoritarian organization.

As indicated in the first chapter, Adorno, *et al.*

(1950) have described the authoritarian personality as excessively aloof, ritualistically attached to routines and procedures, resistant to change, and preoccupied with the rights of authority and status. These authors also report that the authoritarian personality tends to handle his impulses through extensive repressions and countercathexes which hinder ego development. The ego remains rather primitive and isolated from unconscious processes. When the authoritarian personality is confronted with unconscious conflicts he feels shocked and overwhelmed. When his power and authority are threatened, the anxieties of the authoritarian personality may lead to depersonalization, intense repression, denial, displacement, projection, reaction formation, and identification with the aggressor. Other common manifestations of his anxiety can be ethnocentric and sexist behavior.

I wish to point out that defense mechanisms are part of the psychological apparatus of all human beings, irrespective of one's orientation to power, However, the authoritarian personality stands apart from the humanistic personality in that he has a particularly strong predilection for employing certain psychological defense mechanisms more frequently and with greater intensity. Whereas the humanistic personality tends

to deal with his emotional conflicts through, for example, creative work, introspection and humor, the
authoritarian personality involuntarily resorts to
repression, displacement, reaction formation, identification with the aggréssor, and projection. The humanistic personality is also distinguishable from the
authoritarian personality by the former's tendency
to encourage mutual communication and decision-making
in his interpersonal relationships and the latter's
tendency to communicate and make decisions in a unilateral manner.

I will attempt to describe behaviors and attitudes of the Chancellor-Superintendent and his administrative intermediaries and analyze them, within the
context of an institution of higher education, from
the standpoint of how certain psychological defense
mechanisms were actuated in the conflicts between the
college administration and the MHP. The following
descriptions and analyses emanate from my role as a
participant-observer in the MHP. They are derived from
a number of sources, including written documents, my
own personal recollections, and the reports of professional colleagues, such as the Clinical Coordinator
of the MHP.

Repression and Denial

While the MHP was actively consulting with the
Board of Governors, the Governors were also willing, for
the most part, to consult with the MHP. In a speech
to a faculty convocation in 1975, Governor S. expressly
invited the faculty to consult with the Governors on
matters of common concern.

I would conjecture that the Chancellor-Superintendent and the Dean of Students felt betrayed by, and
resentful toward, those Governors who consulted with
and befriended the MHP. For example, on two separate
occasions the Chancellor-Superintendent publicly accused me of "politicizing" the administrative negotiations which affected the MHP. On one of these occasions, he suggested that I was engaging in a form of
lobbying activity which was designed to subvert the
administrative workings of the college and his authority to govern. The Dean of Students reformulated these
allegations in athletic terms when he repeatedly accused me of making "end runs." Neither the Chancellor-
Superintendent nor the Dean ever conceded that the Governors were willing participants and sometimes instig-
ators in a bilateral "politicized" process. Neither
the Chancellor-Superintendent nor the Dean of Students
could acknowledge the discomfiting organizational re-

244

ality that certain Governors felt free to bypass their official authority. Since the Governors were their organizational superiors, the Chancellor-Superintendent and the Dean of Students could not acknowledge or express their feelings of resentment for and to them. Thus, the need for the activation of defense mechanisms, such as repression and denial.

> The repressed consists, first of all, of the ideas and conceptions connected with the aim of the warded-off impulses which, by being warded off, have lost their connection with verbal expression. (Fenichel, 1945, p. 177)

The authoritarian administrator harbors feelings of awe for those in authoritative positions relative to himself. By pedestalling his administrative superiors, he impairs his own capacity to express his feelings, particularly negative feelings, for and to his professional superordinates.

The Chancellor-Superintendent and the Dean of of Students, I would hypothesize, were angered by the receptivity of certain Governors to the MHP and had to psychologically shield themselves from their "forbidden" feelings of rage (to some extent for external, professional reasons) by the mechanisms of repression and denial. The repressed feelings of hostility for the Governors became intensified and they sought verbal and affective outlets elsewhere. I am here conjecturing that the process by which the Chancellor-Superintendent and the Dean of Students psychologically shielded themselves from their own rage was largely unconscious, since a conscious process of concealing one's feelings does not deserve the term "repression."

I think it is appropriate to mention my own reactions to the allegations that I was unilaterally engaging in activities which were disruptive to the college. First, I felt unjustly accused of having engaged in improprieties of any kind. I believed that my lobbying activities were proper and warranted. Consequently, whenever the Dean of Students made inquiries about my unorthodox professional conduct, I readily and guiltlessly admitted that I had sought to influence the Board of Governors.

Second, I deeply resented the inaccurate charge that I was unilaterally negotiating with the Governors. However, I found myself, in this instance, caught in an inextricable bind. I felt victimized by the allegation and wished to legitimize my actions by explaining that I was only as "guilty" of malfeasance as were the Governors. I did not take this tack, however, for several reasons: (1) I believed that it would have given credence to the fallacious notion that I was, indeed, conducting myself unprofessionally, (2) I feared

246

that the Board of Governors would quickly discover that
I was trying to share the "blame" with them and, out of
justifiable resentment, they would disassociate themselves from the MHP and me, (3) I was not sanguine a-
bout the possibility that I could convince the college
administration that my relationship with the Governors
was of a mutual nature; I believed that their perception
of me as a malefactor was too fixed to be modified by
my own interventions, and (4) I have a personal aversion to "passing the buck" when I am confronted with
criticisms about my personal or professional behavior.
Since I thought my actions were consistent with the
ethical tenets of my profession, I preferred to defend them on their own merits. This was temporarily
the more difficult choice for me, since it fastened me
to the conflagrated center of the conflict with the
college administration. However, my uncompromising
stance allowed me to retain a strong measure of personal pride in my convictions and gave me a strengthened determination to carry out my professional objectives.

Displacement

It is significant that the Chancellor-Superintendent, at least within the organizational struc-

ture of the college, vented his anger in a single,
downward direction administratively, i.e., at the MHP
and me.

> The authoritarian *must*, out of inner neces-
> sity, turn his aggression against outgroups.
> He must do so because he is psychologically
> unable to attack ingroup authorities, rather
> than because of intellectual confusion regard-
> ing the sources of his frustration. This
> helps to explain why the aggression can become
> so violent and lose all connection with the
> stimulus which originally set it off.
> (Adorno, *et al.*, 1950, p. 233)

I would conjecture that there were important
political and professional reasons (unknown to me), in
addition to "inner necessities," which caused the
Chancellor-Superintendent to abjure feelings of hostility for the Governors. For example, despite his intense commitment to the success of the County Plan, the
Chancellor-Superintendent stoically acquiesced to the
Governors' defeat of the plan. When Governor F. stated
his reservations about the County Plan, the Chancellor-
Superintendent immediately and silently deferred to
him. He made no attempt to delay the defeat of the
County Plan, nor did he seek to rebut Governor F.'s
reasons for opposing his recommendation. In the face
of Governor F.'s arguments, he appeared cowed and sub-
servient. However, a few minutes later, he vented his
rage at me. He angrily stated, "I have respect for Mr.

248

Amada's (administrative and clinical) work at the college, but I have no respect for the way in which he has politicized this matter."

Dr. L., the Co-Director of the Mt. Zion Crisis Clinic, alludes to another example of the Chancellor-Superintendent's aggression against members of the outgroup:

> In a manner which I considered quite irrational, the Chancellor-Superintendent petulantly asked me why I did not arrange to have my friends at Mt. Zion Hospital subsidize the MHP, since I thought so highly of the program. I told him that I had no authority to carry out such measures. Furthermore, I considered it the responsibility of the Community College District to support the MHP.

The MHP was certainly a "stimulus" for much of the Chancellor-Superintendent's wrath; however, his inability to integrate psychologically the fact that the Governors were "accomplices" in carrying out our program ambitions, caused him to repeatedly level criticisms at the MHP, its supporters, and at me, as "outgroup" members who were causing administrative havoc on the campus. I think that the violence of his anger and the tenacity with which he maintained his resistance to the MHP were directly attributable to the fact that he could not safely express his "inadmissible" feelings of resentment for and to the Board of Governors.

Projection

> Projection is a means of repudiating one's own
> activities and wishes when these become danger-
> ous and of laying the responsibility for them
> at the door of some external agent.
> (Freud, 1966, p. 123)

In our second conference, the Chancellor-Super-

intendent held me blameworthy for circumventing his

authority and employing factious methods of achieving

programmatic ends. He asserted that I had not consult-

ed with him prior to undertaking lobbying activities

to undermine his authority. He stated explicitly that

I had no respect for the established administrative

rules and authorities of the college and that I repre-

sented a serious danger to the institution since, "If

everyone around here decided to do as he pleased, with

complete disregard for rules, we would simply not be

able to carry out our daily responsibility of educat-

ing students" (Ms. Quan Holden).

By taking this tack, the Chancellor-Superintend-

ent "repudiated" his own instrumental role in laying

the groundwork for the unconventional methods to which

he objected. He ascribed to me a penchant for eschew-

ing his authority. By doing so, he psychologically

set aside his rebuffs of the direct and indirect ap-

peals which were made to him for support of the MHP.

He thereby overlooked the palpable link between his

own intransigence and the unconventional activities of the MHP. In effect, he could then absolve himself of unacceptable thoughts that he was a threat to the MHP and perhaps was acting, at least in this instance, against the interests of City College students. I theorize that such unpalatable thoughts were converted into a conception that the real dangerous element on the City College campus was the "external agent," the MHP. Even more dangerous was its personification: I.

The Chancellor-Superintendent's projective tendencies were most evident during our second conference. He had just suffered what was generally considered to be a humiliating loss: the defeat of the County Plan. (For example, immediately following the Board of Governors' meeting in which the County Plan was defeated, a *San Francisco Chronicle* reporter leadingly questioned me as to how I felt about "beating the Chancellor-Superintendent." I refrained from answering the question and, instead, advised the reporter that, in my estimation, newspaper publicity would adversely affect the MHP. Consequently, the *Chronicle* made no mention of the MHP in its coverage of the Board of Governors' meeting the next day.) The Chancellor-Superintendent importuned me to admit that I had incurred a loss. Thus, by projecting his own humiliation onto me, he attempted to

251

salve his own painful feelings of deprivation and loss.

To the best of my knowledge, the Chancellor-Superintendent did not significantly renounce the County Plan after its defeat. As indicated earlier, he "does not feel that permanent staffing is the answer to the problem. He noted that Dr. O. (incoming President) has considerable training in counseling and educational psychology and it is his hope that when he arrives on campus he might establish parameters for this service" (Minutes of the Board of Governors Meeting, 1975).

In my first meeting with President O., he indicated that the Chancellor-Superintendent had no intention of allowing the college to incorporate the MHP. He stated that the Chancellor-Superintendent continued to favor the County Plan; however, since the Board of Governors had refused to adopt that recommendation, the dissolution of the MHP was inevitable. In other words, the Chancellor-Superintendent was willing to totally discard the MHP, unless the County Plan could be resurrected and implemented; an unlikely eventuality. At no point was the Chancellor-Superintendent perceptibly shaken in his conviction that the County Plan was desirable for the MHP and the college. On the other hand, he ceased to actively or publicly expedite its adoption.

The self-contempt of the authoritarian personal-

252

ity produces self-doubts. He bears these doubts by disclaiming responsibility for his failures through projecting them onto others. It is noteworthy that the Dean of Students, who served as the Chancellor-Superintendent's principal intermediary to the MHP, was also one of the organizers of the campus petition drive to mobilize support for the presidential candidacy of the Acting President. Such action was widely regarded as extremely unorthodox and coercive (see earlier comments of the Chairperson of the Personnel Committee of the Academic Senate). Yet the Dean treated his own unorthodoxy as behavior which was within the bounds of administrative propriety. To do otherwise would be to admit unconscious wishes to deviate from or perhaps even subvert established administrative procedures.

The psychological inadmissibility of "extremist" impulses and wishes activates the mechanism of projection. The Dean, therefore, attributed the trait of "extremism" to me and threatened to demand my dismissal for a type of conduct which he found unconsciously enticing and, at the same time, threatening. On at least one occasion, when he resorted to lobbying through the use of circulated petitions, he fell prey to his own "extremist" impulses. This mode of behavior was, however, fundamentally ego-alien, and therefore, had to be renounced and projected. The Dean, as an authoritarian personality, had to project his psychological conflicts onto an administratively weaker entity, namely the MHP. He did this by accusing me on several occasions, of resorting to extremist and divisive behavior.

Identification with the Aggressor

The process of psychological identification occurs in all personalities and all social organizations. The authoritarian personality, however, develops a special pattern of psychological identification.

> Authoritarian personalities often find themselves in complete agreement with the administration of harsh punishment. They identify themselves with the punisher and even seem to enjoy punishment. (Adorno, *et al.*, 1950, p. 351)

The Dean of Students, in my view, was not zealously punitive toward the MHP and me during the first few years of our administrative relationship. However, through the process of identification, he gradually came to emulate the Chancellor-Superintendent's punitive policies and attitudes toward the MHP and me. For example, following my interview with the President's hiring committee, the Dean, with considerable irritation, faulted me for avoiding eye contact with committee members. As indicated earlier, I considered this criticism to be intimidating and vindictive since it was entirely without realistic foundation. Soon after this incident, the Dean berated me for inquiring about my job status with another member of the college administration. He then proceeded to threaten me with expulsion from the college for my "carefree and rebellious end-runs," should they recur. He repeated several times that I was under strict orders not to apprise Ms. Quan Holden of her appointment, despite her ardent wish to be notified of this important information immediately.

I believe the Dean's behavior indicated that he would have sooner suffered pangs of conscience over disloyality to the Chancellor-Superintendent than over mistreatment of the MHP and me. His rather complete "identification with the aggressor" caused him to chastise and threaten me at the very moment when his administrative and spiritual leader had been dealt his most serious psychological blow: my appointment to permanent college employment. His persistent and picayunish concerns about how Ms. Quan Holden was to be notified of her appointment suggested that he was beginning to "enjoy the administration of harsh punishment."

As William Moore (1971) points out, college administrators sometimes solidify their own positions by
placing a person whom they can control in a sensitive
position. In my view, the Dean of Students appointed
the SHS Coordinator to the position of Chairperson of
the two Hiring Committees in order to preordain two
very contrasting outcomes: Ms. U.'s appointment and
my ouster. In addition to any implicit threats which
his authoritative position may have posed to the SHS
Coordinator, the Dean could also depend upon her willingness to identify psychologically with him and his
plans for the MHP.

How the process of psychological identification
affected the actions of the SHS Coordinator was revealed in her comments to Ms. Quan Holden. She first
vaguely indicated that there were "reservations" about
my employment. When asked to divulge the sources of
these "reservations," she (accurately) identified the
Chancellor-Superintendent and the Dean of Students.
She would not, however, clarify or substantiate the
nature of the reservations. When I later confronted
the SHS Coordinator regarding her reservations about
my suitability for permanent employment, she cited an
instance which had occurred in a police science course

several months before. The incident, which she claimed involved the mishandling of a query from a student, was dated, moot, and patently irrelevant, within the context of my qualifications for college employment.

I believe the SHS Coordinator's behavior is explainable when one recognizes that it was largely based upon her psychological identification with the harsh behavior of the Chancellor-Superintendent and the Dean of Students toward the MHP and me. Through her identification and cooperation with these two administrative authorities, the SHS Coordinator had acquired adminitrative positions of considerable influence and prestige (the positions of SHS Coordinator and Chairperson of the Hiring Committees were appointments which were made by the Dean of Students). When she had first revealed reservations about me to Ms. Quan Holden, she had evidently hoped to legitimatize her qualms by referring to the fact that they were also the opinions of the Chancellor-Superintendent and the Dean of Students, administrative authorities with whom she closely identified. When I did not regard such a basis for reservations to be a supportable reason to question my eligibility for college employment, she sought temporary refuge in an obscure classroom incident which occurred several months before. She stated that I had insensitively responded to a student who questioned me in a police science course. She remarked that, on the basis of my uncivil behavior toward that student, she held reservations about my suitability for college employment. I rejoined that such an incident certainly could not outweigh my considerable accomplishments in the MHP. I also expressed my belief that she was brandishing the incident as a "red herring," in order to conceal other, more duplicitous reasons for opposing my employment. The SHS Coordinator replied that my incredulity reflected an immature aversion to accepting criticism. She stated that it was this trait which made it very difficult to work compatibly with me. I again expressed my disbelief in her statements and then threatened to take legal action in order to gain fair access to college employment. The discussion ended at that point.

Reaction Formation

The perception of instinctual dangers, such as the unexpected eruption of intense rage, can result in rigid and cramped attitudes which hinder the expression of impulses. Such attitudes, when sufficiently unmasked, will reveal that opposite attitudes still reside in the unconscious. The manifest attitudes are

258

called reaction formations.

The authoritarian personality maintains a "tough-ness" as a reaction formation against unconscious feel-ings of weakness and tenderness. In the case of the Chancellor-Superintendent, I hypothesize that his re-lentless and tenacious resistance to the MHP and me was, in part, a psychological defense against feelings of insecurity and powerlessness. On one occasion, when he was re-emphasizing his view that the MHP would not become a college program, he remarked that he did not wish to appear "hard-nosed." I believe that he was here manifesting an attitude which was quite contrary to his unconscious concerns; namely, that one might regard him as appearing, to continue in the context of the anatomical metaphor, "spineless."

I conjecture that the Chancellor-Superintend-ent's tremendous emotional investment and demonstra-tion of administrative power in resisting the MHP and me were based upon unconscious feelings of dread that any compromise with the MHP, particularly after the conflicts became heated, would be construed as a sign of personal weakness. His decision to maintain a tough administrative posture by refusing to "nego-tiate with (rank-and-file) staff" was, I believe, more a reflection of self-doubts about his personal strength than an adherence to established administrative practice. At that point he could not allow empathic feelings to rule his judgment. As an authoritarian personality, he feared that any empathically motivated attempt to compromise with the MHP would mark him as a weak leader.

What empirical evidence is available to suggest that the Chancellor-Superintendent bore compassionate feelings for the MHP and me? The defense mechanism of reaction formation is subtle and becomes identifiable only when "secondary" defensive attitudes begin to crumble and are eclipsed by the "primary" attitudes of the unconscious. When the Chancellor-Superintendent abetted us to recruit MHP positions from other college departments, he was not idly recommending a "wild goose chase." Ms. Quan Holden and I perceived the Chancellor-Superintendent's recommendation as a supportive and authentic attempt to extricate the MHP from an otherwise impossible dilemma. I would conjecture that the Chancellor-Superintendent momentarily hoped that the MHP would be rescued by an adminitrative contrivance which would protect him from his deepest dread: the fear of appearing powerless and "losing face." When the plan failed, however, he could not allow compassion to dictate an independent adminsitrative resolve to favor permanent adoption of the MHP without incurring self-recriminations over feelings of powerlessness. Rather than bear such repellent feelings, he warded them off by reverting to a "powerful" resistance to the MHP and me.

Social and Behavioral Characteristics of the Authoritarian Personality

I will now consider two social and behavioral characteristics of the authoritarian personality which, I believe, were exhibited by the Chancellor-Superintendent and his administrative supporters in their interactions with the MHP: sexism and racism.

Sexism

According to Adorno, *et al.*, authoritarian personalities tend to view mother figures (women) as sacrificing and submissive. Such personalities hold a conception of father figures (men) as distant, stern, dominant and sometimes psychopathic. The following is a dynamic explanation of the authoritarian personality's conception of the opposite sex: "There is an ambivalent underlying disrespect for, and resentment against, the opposite sex, often hidden behind an externalized and excessive pseudoadmiration" (Adorno, *et al.*, 1950, p. 399).

In what respect did such conceptions affect the Chancellor-Superintendent's behavior toward the MHP? Most of the lobbying activities used to impede the administrative staff from imposing the County Plan were planned and implemented by Ms. Quan Holden and me, acting in concert. Yet I was consistently perceived as an aggressively plotting malefactor and Ms. Quan Holden as a passive onlooker in the conflict between the MHP and the college administration. It was not conceivable to the Chancellor-Superintendent and his administrative supporters that Ms. Quan Holden, as a woman, could boldly aggress against their policies and practices. As a result, their conscious hostility remained focused upon the only (male) person who could, in their estimation, possess dominant and aggressive qualities: me.

The relative immunity from criticisms which was afforded Ms. Quan Holden by the college administration was not based upon a genuine appreciation or liking for her considerable personal and professional qualities. Rather it was founded upon (in Ms. Quan Holden's view and mine) a disrespect, actually a contempt, for her capacity to demonstrate nonconformist and aggressive qualities. The authoritarian personality associates such qualities only with maleness

and blinds himself to feminine aggressiveness, even
when its manifestations are obvious.

I think it is relevant to mention here the
psychological effects of the college administration's
sexist attitude upon Ms. Quan Holden and me. Since
I rather exclusively bore the brunt of the college administration's criticisms, I often felt scapegoated
and, therefore, resentful toward Ms. Quan Holden because of her relatively protected position. On the
other hand, this same social phenomenon caused me to
be unduly credited for our joint success in overcoming the college administration's opposition. This, of
course, rankled Ms. Quan Holden. However, the cohe-
sive and candid relationship which Ms. Quan Holden and
I maintained throughout our administrative struggles
prevented these factors from rending our alliance and
the MHP.

Racism

A primary characteristic of the authoritarian
personality is an ethnocentric ideology which leads
to a general rejection of outgroups.

> It is as if the ethnocentric individual feels
> threatened by most of the groups to which he
> does not have a sense of belonging; if he can-
> not identify, he must oppose; if a group is not
> "acceptable," it is "alien." The ingroup-out-
> group distinction thus becomes the basis for

most of his social thinking, and people are
categorized primarily according to which groups
they belong. (Adorno, *et al.*, 1950, p. 147)

The categorization of outgroups results in ster-

eotypical conceptions which make it impossible for

the ethnocentrist to approach individuals *as* indivi-

duals. There is a tendency to prejudge each indivi-

dual "only as a sample specimen of the reified group"

(Adorno, *et al.*, 1950).

How did the Chancellor-Superintendent and his

administrative subordinates display ethnocentric think-

ing and behavior? Largely, by regarding and treating

Ms. Quan Holden in a manner consistent with their

stereotypical conceptions of Asians, particularly of

Asian women.

> The Asian-American woman bears the burden of a
> double onus: she must be an Asian-American
> and a female. In striving for success and
> positions of leadership, the female must work
> harder than the male in proving her capabili-
> ties. For most women, their idea of "femin-
> inity" -- being supportive followers -- pre-
> vents them from seeking power over other men
> and women. The Asian-American woman is taught
> from birth that she is inferior in quality to
> her male counterpart; inferior in ability, in-
> telligence, perception, and emotional stability.
> "Brainwashed" through mass media stereotyping
> and interactions with family and friends, she
> concludes that, to be feminine and desirable,
> she must be passive, submissive and contented.
> By attempting to expand her life space to in-
> clude personal feelings, individuality, and
> creativity, she risks being labelled and
> treated as "unfeminine" or "castrating." The
> labelling is done by various groups, sexists

264

and racists, and even by those in the Asian-
American movement. (Fujitomi & Wong, 1973,
p. 260)

The Chancellor-Superintendent and his organizational intermediaries, on the basis of stereotypical conceptions, associated aggressive traits with
me because I am White, and submissive characteristics
with Ms. Quan Holden because she is Asian. Therefore,
allegations of extremism and politicalization were
directed solely at me, since Ms. Quan Holden could
not be acknowledged to have the "individuality" and
"creativity" to engage in such modes of behavior.
Even when Ms. Quan Holden openly made disclaimers of
inaction and passivity in her administrative dealings
with the college administration, she was not approached
as an individual. As a "sample specimen of the reified group," she was seen as a supportive follower
rather than as a unique individual who possessed aggressive and creative capabilities. By maintaining
this attitude toward Ms. Quan Holden, the Chancellor-
Superintendent and his administrative subordinates
could ward off their unconscious contempt for a fe-
male Asian who behaved, according to their concept-
tions, in an "unfeminine" and "castrating" manner.

In my opinion, there were two reasons why ethnocentrism also influenced the college adminstration's

265

attitude toward me. First, my professional work, both within the MHP as well as with the Westside Community Mental Health Services, clearly identified me as a strong proponent of the rights of minority groups. The college administration had, for many years, been dilatory in dealing effectively with the need for increased minority representation of its staff. Many departments throughout the college, including, for example, the academic nursing and counseling programs, had long been underrepresented by minority professionals. Since I outspokenly advocated, and perennially succeeded in achieving, at least in the MHP, an ethnically balanced staff, I was undoubtedly viewed as a vexatious gadfly by the college administration, which tended to complacently regard its own gradual strides in the hiring of minority staff as a record of substantial success.

The following example, I believe, illustrates my point. Each semester I sent the roster of the MHP staff, including its ethnic breakdown, to the entire Counseling Department staff. In 1976, I received a reply from one of the counselors, who circled the column which listed the ethnic backgrounds of the MHP staff and wrote, in the margin, "Who are you kidding? This is phony." He did not sign his reply, evidently

266

wishing to remain anonymous. I took the reply to a
dean with whom I had a mutually trusting relationship.
She stated that there were several members of the
Counseling Department who were capable of such "racist bullshit." She went on to say that the college
administration had respected and protected those counselors for many years, allowing them to behave, with
impunity, in a discriminatory manner. She referred
me to another (Black) dean, who philosophically chuck-
led over the incident. The matter, evidently, was
given no further administrative consideration.

Second, I believe that my being a Jew and originally from the East Coast was significant to the
college administration's negative perception of me.
The Chancellor-Superintendent and the Dean of Students
are native Californians of Catholic background. I
think the geographical and ethnic contrast between
us accounted, in part, for why I have been viewed as
an "extremist" member of an outgroup. I would conjecture that the Catholicism of the Chancellor-Superintendent and the Dean of Students was one factor
which contributed to their overriding reverence for
established, hierarchical authority. To a considerable extent, I considered my own skeptical, somewhat
irreverent attitude toward established authority to

be a product of my East Coast, Jewish heritage. For this reason, I regarded the college administration's characterization of my behavior as "extremist," to constitute a form of ethnic and regional prejudice.

Characteristics of the Authoritarian Organization

The impact of growth and specialization has imparted to modern organizations certain authoritarian or "bureaupathic" qualities. I will analyze the interactions between the college administration and the MHP by using the theoretical framework of Thompson (1971).

Within the authoritarian organization there are many sources of conflict and insecurity. In such organizations insecurity is induced by the inordinate stress placed upon satisfying and conforming to the wishes of the highest administrative authorities. Administrative underlings, whose own status and importance depend largely upon meeting the often subjective standards of the "boss," will develop intense feelings of self-doubt over their professional competency. In an authoritarian system, one assesses his value to the organization according to his perception of how much his superiors appreciate or promote him, rather than base his worth upon the quality of his profes-

sional performance *per se*. Personal security hinges
upon the discretion of one or very few authorities and
there is a repetitive and almost automatic adherence
to administrative directives and policies.

A second source of insecurity within the authoritarian organization is described as follows:

> The person in a hierarchical position tends to
> be caught on the horns of a dilemma. He must
> satisfy the nonexplicit and nonoperational de-
> mands of a superior through the agency of spe-
> cialized subordinates and nonsubordinates whose
> skills he only dimly understands. And yet, to
> be counted a success he must accept this di-
> lemma and live with its increasing viciousness
> throughout his life. He must live with in-
> creasing insecurity and anxiety. Given a per-
> son's hierarchical relationship with his su-
> perior, he is always subject to blame for out-
> comes which he could control only remotely, if
> at all. (Thompson, 1971, p. 470)

The role and conduct of the Dean of Students
amply demonstrate how the anxiety to satisfy a superi-
or administrative authority promoted a single-minded
adherence to the wishes and directives of that authority.

Throughout the college administration's pursuit
of the County Plan, the Dean avoided or discouraged all
discussion of alternatives to that plan. Since his own
status and prestige depended upon the efficient execu-
tion of the Chancellor-Superintendent's orders, he felt
an understandable aversion to any critical evaluations

269

of the validity and consequences of those orders. When
Ms. Quan Holden and I countermanded the Chancellor-
Superintendent's plans, we were, in effect, threatening
the Dean's security. In such a situation, the Dean
had two broad choices: (1) to re-examine and perhaps
modify the Chancellor-Superintendent's proposals for
the MHP, or (2) to accelerate and intensify the execu-
tion of his superior's orders. Within the framework of
the authoritarian structure of the college, however,
such a choice did not realistically exist. The resolution of the conflict had to be made by imposing upon
the weaker administrative unit (the MHP) the wishes of
the most powerful administrative authority.

The Dean of Students was surely on the "horns
of a dilemma." He had no doubt hoped to enlist the
cooperation of the MHP in achieving his superordinate's
objectives. He admitted many times to Ms. Quan Holden
and me that he "only dimly" understood the specialized
nature of our work. Since he was operating in an
authoritarian milieu, he necessarily ruled out the
possibility of trusting and supporting the proposals
of his administrative subordinates. Nor could he allow
himself the luxury of patiently acquiring a fuller understanding of the rationales of our position. He
was painfully aware of the fact that he would be blamed

for "outcomes which he could control only remotely, if
at all." His insecurity in this dilemma fostered an
even more "patriotic" pursuit of his administrative
superior's orders.

The Drift to Quantitative Compliance

The authoritarian organization fosters an exaggerated dependence upon regulations and quantitative
standards. For example, the Dean of Students rarely
inquired about the clinical skills, assignments or
accomplishments of the psychological trainees in the
MHP; on the other hand, he repeatedly and warningly inquired about the quantity of time which the MHP staff
were allotting to the supervision of the trainees. A-
other of his preoccupations with quantitative compliance became a source of some hilarity among the SHS
staff. The Dean would punctually telephone various
SHS staff in the very beginning minutes of their work
day, ask several bogus questions, and appear quite indifferent to their replies.

The efficiency of the authoritarian organization
appears to rest upon its ability to control subordinates through the imposition of myriad rules and regulations.

> Where the need to control exists, it often man-
> ifests itself in procedures, reports, and clear-

> ances governing trivia, while at the same time
> very important matters are left to discretion
> because controlling them is not feasible. The
> need to control is sufficiently widespread to
> have given sometimes a petty and ludicrous qual-
> ity to modern organization. (Thompson, 1971,
> p. 471)

The authoritarian administration of City College

placed great emphasis upon quantitative compliance and,

consequently, effected the trivialization of important

matters. For example, the Chancellor-Superintendent,

frustrated by his inability to control the MHP and me,

raised objections to my off-campus private psychother-

apy practice. Such work arrangements were common and

licit on the City College campus. Prior to our suc-

cessful resistance to the County Plan, there had been

no implication that my private practice was questiona-

ble. However, since I had become perceived by the ad-

ministration as administratively elusive and uncontrol-

lable, a "trivial" point was introduced in order to

cast doubts upon my willingness to comply with organi-

zational regulations. In the authoritarian setting

of the college, a realistic qualitative assessment of

my professional work was not considered relevant or

necessary. However, if it could be documented that I

was falling short of quantitative standards, perhaps

I would suffer personal insecurities and comport my-

self in a more accomodating manner.

272

The emphasis upon quantitative compliance emerged most transparently at the juncture when the Chancellor-Superintendent and the Dean of Students considered themselves least in control of the MHP and me. In August, 1976, I learned that Ms. Quan Holden and I had been selected by the President for the two permanent MHP positions which were newly established by the college. I sought confirmation of this information from the Dean of Students. He brusquely acknowledged that we had been appointed. At that point there were several important issues which warranted discussion between us. For example, Ms. Quan Holden and I were ignorant of the administrative procedures which would ultimately lead to our being hired. As indicated earlier, we unsuspectingly discovered that it was crucial for us to attend the Board of Governors' meeting, at which we were to be officially hired. Yet the Dean avoided and inhibited all discussion of such vital practical matters. Instead, he used the opportunity of our encounter to impose his own impromptu regulation which prohibited me from notifying Ms. Quan Holden of her appointment. Several months later, when I expressed my resentment to him for such hectoring behavior, he first denied that he had acted autocratically toward me. He then asserted, by way of self-justification, that such matters (job appointments) were commonly communicated only through official channels and, therefore his treatment of me was not untoward or extraordinary. I believe this incident illustrated the Dean's viewpoint that if I could not be impeded or controlled through a qualitative evaluation of my professional performance, I would be stymied by a strict application of "trivial" and "ludicrous" regulations.

Organizational Resistances to the Establishment of College Mental Health Services

The organizers and administrators of college mental health services should expect to encounter multifarious and strong resistances to the establishment of their programs. The organizational resistances to which I will refer are, I believe, universal and predictable throughout colleges and universities, irrespective of their geographic, political, administrative or ethnic characteristics.

At this point, I would like to remind the reader that, although I will, as indicated earlier, stress the role of institutional and personal resistances to mental health services, the majority of City College personnel, in my view, strongly and gen-

erously support the MHP (recall the earlier reference
to the fact that the MHP, in the midst of its most
serious crisis, received the largest outporing of mail
and telephone support in the history of the college.

The Polarized Social and Political Perceptions of
Mental Health Services

Two, quite polarized perceptions of mental health
services develop on the college campus, sometimes serenely cohabiting the mind of a single individual. One
point of view is that the mental health service is an
insidious, clandestine, and even subversive organizational entity. At this end of the perceptual spec-
trum, mental health services are viewed as the champions
of sexual libertinism, irreligiousity, and indiscrimi-
nate nonconformity. The policy of confidentiality which
the service maintains is considered further evidence of
nefarious goings-on. Consequently, those who work in
the mental health service tend to be viewed as amoral,
anarchistic and untrustworthy.

For example, in one of my earliest meetings with
the Counseling Department, a counselor queried, "Why is
it that you don't want to talk with us, or won't tell
us anything about what you do in the Mental Health Program?" Smiling, I parried the question by saying, "Do

275

you mean do I *still* beat my wife?" I then asked him to elaborate on his reasons for thinking that we did not wish to discuss our work with counselors. He stated that the MHP's policy of confidentiality raised "certain" suspicions about the nature of our work.

I assured the counselor that the client-psycho-therapist relationship was confidential only because students preferred, insisted upon, and deserved such protection of their privacy. The counselor retorted that he believed the policy of confidentiality indicated that the MHP staff were self-servingly worried that their professional colleagues would discover "something about how you really work with students." He added that he saw no particular reason for a policy of confidentiality, other than to provide a "cover" for professional improprieties. The counselor did not spell out what he meant by the word "improprieties;" however, I believe he was implying that the MHP was furtively fostering antisocial and aberrant behavior in students.

At the other end of the perceptual continuum, the mental health service is viewed as a rich font of miraculous "cures." This viewpoint emanates from the tendency of some college personnel to impute godlike attributes to the mental health service. Because the

276

psychological problems of students are often perplexing and provocative to the college staff, there is a concomitant wish that they be resolved without delays or complications. This wish is then transformed into a genuine expectation of the MHP, which has already been psychologically endowed with omnipotent powers.

For example, I was once introduced to a class by a Health Education instructor in the following manner: This is Dr. Amada. He's a terrific person to see if you have any personal problems. He instantaneously cures students." I was stunned by the introduction and I closely examined the tone and content of the instructor's comments for signs of irony or levity. Unfortunately, I found none. I then proceeded to point out to the class that, although I had helped many students, there was no such thing as a psychological "cure." Obviously, expectations of "instantaneous cures" will result in excessive disappointment and disillusionment. The mental health service may then be subject to false accusations that it is misrepresenting its value to students.

The polarized perceptions of the MHP, to a great extent, reflect the psychological phenomenon of transference. The program represents, in this case, either the "good" parent who succors and heals, or the "bad" parent who rejects, foments disorder or secretly plans mischief. I will return to the subject of psychological transference as a source of resistance to the MHP later in this discussion.

The Role of Psychological Deprivation as a Resistance to Mental Health Services

The provision of mental health services to students often meets with the intense ambivalence of college personnel. The staff of a college sometimes harbor rivalrous feelings toward its students. When the mental health service extends help to students, these rivalrous emotions will become intensified. The program is then perceived as the "bad" parent who "plays favorites," i.e., wholeheartedly nurtures "undeserving siblings" and thereby deprives others.

Since the academic institution cannot meet all of the emotional and social needs of its employees, many staff predictably turn to the mental health services for psychological sustenance. Occasionally, the program can successfully meet the emotional needs of distressed colleagues. However, because the service is primarily designed for students, college staff frequently feel deprived emotionally by the program, since their own psychological needs must be deferred

and met elsewhere. This sense of emotional deprivation may become a basis for resentment and virulent
opposition toward the mental health service.

Several examples will illustrate the role of
emotional deprivation as a basis for resistance to
mental health services. I have been introduced to
many classes, usually by instructors who were enthusiastic supporters of the MHP, in the following manner: Dr. Amada works for a fine program. Don't for-
get, the program is free. You know, when I had to
receive my private psychotherapy, I had to pay a hell
of a lot of money. You people (students) are lucky,
you don't pay anything. And it's right here, at your
convenience." Instructors who openly acknowledge and
express such envy, in my opinion, generally are able
to maintain a positive attitude toward the MHP. However, when such feelings are repressed or denied, they
may fester and eventually find ill-disguised expression in opposition to the MHP.

For example, in a meeting with the Counseling
Department, a counselor whom I hardly knew unexpectedly
challenged the validity of an on-campus mental health
service. There was, at that moment, little opportunity
for a constructive dialogue between us, so I arranged
to meet privately with him afterward. In the privacy

of his office he enunciated his reasons for opposing the MHP. He remarked sharply, "Your program coddles students. You give them more help than they want or need. This is a college, not a grade school. These students are adults and must stand on their own feet. *I didn't get such help when I went to college, and I got by. Why should they get more than I got?"*

This counselor's sense of personal deprivation and rage was glaringly triggered by the psychological "coddling" of students by the MHP. His opposition to the program, when viewed in this light, was therefore understandable and inevitable.

A third example of the role of psychological deprivation as a basis for opposition to the MHP took place in a meeting of the entire Student Health Service staff. Ms. Quan Holden had described a highly successful meeting which she had held with a group of student peer counselors. Her comments included specific examples of how she had effectively assisted the peer counselors during their meeting. At the conclusion of her remarks, one of the SHS nurses responded by saying, "You know, I wish you were able to do for us what you just did for the peer counselors. We need that kind of help here too. I feel jealous." And sorely deprived too, I believe.

The Need for Perfection: The "Emperor's Clothes"
Syndrome

The authoritarian college administration fears
that the mere existence of an on-campus mental health
service is intrinsic proof of the imperfections of the
academic institution. Authoritarian college administrations, in particular, are wont to minimize or conceal the imperfections and dysfunctionings of their
institutions. Although they may not depict their
schools in utopian terms, authoritarian college administrators admit only grudgingly that their schools are
beset by many complicated and sometimes insoluble problems. A major reason for this concealment and dissimulation is a dread that they will be held personally responsible for unsatisfactory results, even when
the outcomes which cause their concern are actually
outside their sphere of influence.

A mental health service can be perceived as a
clarion pronouncement that "all is not well" on the
college campus. The program bespeaks of the fact that
there are dissatisfied, troubled and even severely
disturbed students attending the college. A logical
inference may be drawn from the need for a mental
health service, that students are not having all of
their psychological needs met elsewhere on the campus,

such as in classrooms, counseling sessions, or through athletic activities. This inference may affront the college administration which strives to maintain an image of administrative perfection. It may then suffer irrational fears of being accused of neglecting, in the "academic programs," the emotional needs of students. Even worse, it may fear that it will somehow be charged with being the principal culprit which is fostering the psychological turmoil of students.

If the mental health program demonstrates *its* value by identifying and assisting dissatisfied or unhappy students, and the college administration demonstrates *its* value by documenting how satisfied and contented are its students, a conflict must ensue. The college administration will attempt to disprove the contention that appreciable numbers of students are in need of psychological help. One means of achieving this end is to oppose the growth of the MHP. According to this tortuous but prevalent reasoning, a mental health service which is small and without influence denotes that there are few students who require such a program. If few students require such services, so goes this reasoning, the college administration must be outstandingly successful in meeting all of the emotional needs of students. In its crudest form,

282

this reasoning leads to the fantastic belief that a successful mental health program "means" an unsuccessful college administration, and vice versa.

The college administration's striving for perfection and its correlative dread of losing its "emperor's clothes" were particularly evident immediately following the publication in a local newspaper of a health survey of the student population of City College. The findings of this survey, which, incidentally, were entirely consistent with the findings of most epidemiological research dealing with the City of San Francisco, suggested that City College students generally suffered from a considerable number of physical and psychological disorders, many of which were serious. Immediately following the publication of the survey, one of its authors received a telephone call from the Chancellor-Superintendent, who proceeded to charge him with needlessly tarnishing the image of the college. He was also told that his research methods were unscientific and his findings inaccurate. The Chancellor-Superintendent's verbal onslaught ended with the allegation that the entire matter "made me look bad."

The reader is here reminded of my earlier comments regarding the health status of the citizens of the city of San Francisco, from which the student popu-

283

lation of City College is drawn. For example, although cirrhosis of the liver is the seventh leading cause of death nationally, this disease is the fifth leading cause of death in the city of San Francisco. Suicide is the seventh leading cause of death in San Francisco, as compared to its tenth rank nationally. Certainly, one cannot reasonably hold the Chancellor-Superintendent responsible, as he himself seemed to do, for the significant numbers of City College students who are alcoholic or suicide-prone.

The Fear of Exposure, as a Resistance to Mental Health Services

The college mental health service is often perceived, with a degree of validity, as a pipeline to otherwise secret information. Because the divulgence of private and sometimes highly controversial matters is often psychotherapeutic, and is protected by a policy of confidentiality, the mental health service becomes a willing receptacle for many of the inner secrets of the college.

In all colleges there are varying degrees of indiscrete or unprofessional behavior, as well as outright delinquent conduct, among the staff. Sometimes sexual peccadilloes, for example, conflict with the role of the professional academician. The mental health service learns (or is believed to learn) of many of these matters through its intensive interviews with students. In some instances, students construct imaginings about the misconduct of college personnel which are obviously without foundation in reality. In other instances, students have indisputable proof of the errant behavior of the staff.

Occasionally, one can recognize the gnawing distrust which the MHP induces in the college community by its willingness to learn the "secrets" of students. For example, I have many times been asked by instructors such questions as, "I guess you hear a lot of stories about how students don't like, or feel messed up by, their instructors, huh?" I normally answer such questions by saying that students generally speak to us in positive terms about their instructors; which is largely true. Nevertheless, to the extent that certain college personnel consider themselves guilty of unprofessional conduct, they may suspect that the MHP is the recipient of information which is potentially damaging to their careers. Such suspicions may create irrational fears of exposure by the MHP which, in turn, will become a basis for resistance to the presence of an on-campus mental health service.

Territoriality as a Resistance to Mental Health Services

As indicated earlier in the paper, those who
work in modern organizations tend to regard their professional facilities and prerogatives as the amenities
of their personal fiefdom. As a result, there is always a degree of concern about territorial encroachment.
Some of this concern is over the possible misappropria-
tion of property or physical territory. This may be
accompanied by a dread that others within the organization, especially those with superior ambitions and
abilities, will provide services which will invalidate
and replace their own professional services.

Mental health services have no monopoly on the
meeting of the emotional needs of students. Students'
emotional needs are constantly dealt with by a wide
range of college personnel throughout the campus. Many
academic counselors and instructors legitimately spend
considerable amounts of time with students who wish
to discuss their personal concerns and feelings. Obviously, not all students who feel emotionally upset
are suitable candidates for formal psychotherapeutic
services. Many, quite sensibly, prefer to share their
intimate thoughts with instructors or counselors whom

they already know and trust, than turn to a psychotherapist who is a complete stranger to them.

Nevertheless, there is a widespread concern which, I believe, diminishes each successive year at City College, that the MHP will erode or usurp the prerogatives of other college personnel who wish to engage students in discussions of a personal nature. Recall the comments of the former City College President: "There was a degree of apprehension at the college that the institution of the MHP would constitute a jurisdictional invasion of the Counseling Department." Although this "invasion" never materialized, there continued to be some "apprehension" that the staff of the MHP would, monopolistically, frown upon the psychological interventions of those who worked in other programs.

The concerns which some segments of the college community harbor, that the MHP will devour their professional prerogatives to intervene psychologically with students, are not entirely without basis. For example, an instructor was consulted by one of his students who was in serious conflict with her rather punitive parents. His first inclination was to talk extensively and painstakingly with the student about her concerns. In a short time, the student's problems

287

grew worse, despite the instructor's assistance. The instructor finally turned to me for help.

I told the instructor that I would be willing to help the student directly. When asked my opinion as to what role he should maintain with the student, I suggested that he support her involvement in psychotherapy and attempt to focus his discussions with her upon academic matters. This appeared to be satisfactory to him. The instructor referred the student to me and after I had seen her twice, she had a serious clash with her parents. She fled from her home, traveled to the city in which the instructor lived and called him in a state of desperation. She had no money or shelter for the evening. What the instructor did in response this student's crisis is, I believe, highly relevant to the point under discussion. Rather than call me to consult about how we might best proceed (I am usually easily reached at home or through my answering service), he discarded our agreement by offering the student personal advice. He recommended that she seek shelter in a nearby hostel. The student followed his advice, went to the hostel, and attached herself to a man there who had exhibited an immediate interest in her. She submissively left the hostel with him later in the evening, ostensibly to

288

see a movie, and eventually was raped by him on a dark-
ened side street. In a subsequent talk with the instructor he admitted, without prompting from me, that
he should have consulted me before advising the student
that traumatic evening. This example illustrates the
resistance which some college personnel have to relin-
quishing to the MHP their prerogatives to attend to the
psychological needs of students, even when such re-
linquishment may be necessary.

There are instances when the MHP is called
upon to supercede or usurp the prerogatives of other
college personnel, despite the inadvisability of
such action. For example, I participated, with several instructors, a dean, and a counselor, in a conference which was called to determine whether a dental hygiene student should be retained in that program. Although I did not know the student, based upon
the reports of the other participants, I recommended
strongly that she be dropped from the program and be
given an opportunity to graduate by taking courses in
other programs. This student had a positive, long-
standing relationship with the counselor, who recommended that she be retained in the program. My recommendation was enthusiastically endorsed by the instructors and was eventually adopted.

The discussion next turned to the subject of how to tactfully inform the student of the adverse decision and the need for someone to commiserate with her expected disappointment. One of the instructors urged that I undertake that responsibility. I immediately noticed that the counselor grimaced at this suggestion. I replied that the counselor had far better credentials than I for such an assignment, since he knew the student well and she trusted him. With some relief, I thought, the counselor eagerly volunteered to talk with the student. He and I left the conference on positive terms with each other, despite our contrary recommendations.

The above-mentioned examples illustrate how a mental health service may be viewed as a threat to the territorial prerogatives of the college community. The perception of real or imagined imperilment to one's territorial prerogatives can become a basis for strong resistances to on-campus mental health services.

Economic Considerations as a Resistance to Mental Health Services

Throughout the history of the MHP, economic considerations were injected into the discussions a-

bout the expansion and/or adoption of the program.
These considerations were raised for a number of valid
reasons. The community college district budgets its
various programs with finite financial resources. The
adoption of the MHP, which resulted from establishing
two tenured positions, will become a very expensive
investment. Including the cost of a secretary and at
least two part-time psychotherapists, the program will
cost almost $50,000 a year. Assuming the program con-
tinues only until the end of this century, which actually predates the mandatory retirement ages of Ms.
Quan Holden and me, the projected cost of the MHP is
over one million dollars for the twenty-year period.
Expenditures of such proportions certainly serve as
causes for resistance to the incorporation of such
programs.

It is usually impossible to offer ironclad proof
of the cost effectiveness of mental health services.
Consequently, it is likely that the authoritarian college administration will regard psychological services as a costly luxury or frill. For example, prior
to the final adoption of the MHP, I mentioned to the
Dean of Business Affairs that the MHP helped students
to remain in college, thereby bolstering State reim-
bursements to the college. I also enumerated the many

dangerous and potentially costly incidents which the MHP had skillfully quenched on the campus over the years. He impatiently replied, "There is no way you (the MHP) can prove that you were the pivotal factor in helping a student continue here. There might be a million other intervening reasons for such a decision by a student. The same holds true for those emergencies. How do we know whether they might have been as well handled by personnel we already have in our employ? What I do know is that I have only so much money to spend in this office, and your program is damned expensive." (This episode is reminiscent of the quip attributed to Sigmund Freud, "that the best control is to treat the same person twice - once with analysis and once without, and then compare results." If it were really necessary to apply such rigorous and illusory standards and controls to college mental health services in order to prove their efficacy, value and cost-effectiveness, mental health administrators would be hopelessly hamstrung in adequately defending their programs.)

Economic considerations often have a tendency to develop into veritable alarums. The college administration, in order to resist the costly growth of the mental health service, may begin to describe the program as one which will unimpededly evolve into an administrative colossus and eventually drain the college district of funds which are essential to other educational programs. For example, recall the asseverations of the Chancellor-Superintendent: "If funds such as these are transferred to this program (MHP) it would mean establishment of a priority and service which in actuality should be available to every adult in San Francisco because every adult in San Francisco is a potential student. If the service is available at City College, then it should also be available at all the Community College Centers" (Minutes of the Board of Governors Meeting, June, 1975). In this statement, the Chancellor-Superintendent formulates futuristic economic considerations in order to resist the incorporation of the MHP.

Interpersonal Expectations as Resistances to Mental Health Services

As indicated earlier, the presence of an on-campus mental health service, particularly one which is viewed as a highly authoritative resource of the college, induces perceptible transference reactions in college personnel. The program, as a result, activates in the college community those strong infantile wishes which were originally harbored in relation to one's parents. For example, it is not unusual to detect indications in co-workers of a genuine conviction that the mental health staff have omniscient and omnipotent powers. A corollary of this conviction is the magical belief that those who practice psychotherapy can actually "see through" others. Naturally, such beliefs cause one to feel psychologically transparent and highly vulnerable in his relations with the psychotherapist.

The "parental" aura which often surrounds a college mental health program may incite highly charged emotions towards its staff. Infantile longings and fears may cause segments of the college community to perceive the program as a paragon of perfection and beneficence. There is often an underlying contempt which accompanies such a distorted viewpoint, and this contempt sometimes surfaces when the mental health program reveals its disappointing shortcomings and imperfections.

The transference attitudes which are animated by a mental health service can have many and sometimes subtle implications for the interpersonal relationships which develop between its staff and the rest of the college community. The mental health staff may be approached on an interpersonal basis as if they were larger-than-life, all-knowing and bounteous personages. In this case, they may be treated with adulation and obsequiousness. This places immeasurable interpersonal hardships upon the mental health staff which may feel it incumbent upon themselves to repeatedly and even ostentatiously give evidence of their own doubts and weaknessess: i.e., their humanness.

Other members of the academic community may have quite dissimilar interpersonal reactions to their transference feelings about the mental health program. Since their ego-ideal may be the perfectly integrated personality, who remains impervious to the human conflicts of everyday life, this segment of the college community may become enraged and embittered over the willingness of the mental health service to become embroiled in mundane campus affairs, such as acquisitive budgetary struggles. This group commonly expects that the staff of the mental health service will always work harmoniously with others and communicate only in unemotional, self-controlled and even ascetic terms. In other words, they expect that members of the mental health staff will conduct themselves with their professional colleagues, very much as they might do in their psychotherapeutic sessions with students.

The interpersonal resistances to the MHP were very evident in the relationship between the college administration and the MHP. For example, after a meeting in which I described the machinations of the college administration to thwart the MHP as "disgraceful," I was told by the Dean of Students that as a "psychologist" I should know better than to use such inflammatory language. "Why can't you control yourself better," the Dean is reported to have asked me exasperatedly (Ms. Quan Holden, 1977). In another interpersonal situation, the Chancellor-Superintendent chastised me for flouting his authority. He then proceeded to describe me as a psychological expert who should appreciate the value of following established rules and procedures. In discussing the recent Board of Governors meeting, he interpreted the Board's decision to veto the County Plan as my failure and then importuned me to admit my loss by saying, "As a psychologist you should know the value of admitting such feelings. So go ahead, admit it, you lost" (Ms. Quan Holden). This interpersonal treatment was justified on the grounds that I, as a psychological expert, would understand and appreciate the need for a cathartic expression of feeling.

When Ms. Quan Holden and I would admit to the

Dean that the persistent conflicts with the college administration were causing us extreme psychological stress, he would derisively comment in the following manner: "You're under stress, huh? I thought you people knew how to handle stress. I didn't think you allowed yourself to get upset or bothered like other people. You shouldn't, you know. You have the knowledge and skills to deal with these problems, without getting disturbed."

The above-mentioned examples illustrate the admixture of awe and contempt which characterized the interpersonal responses of many college personnel to a mental health staff. These responses were frequently based upon transference attitudes which were activated by the mental health services to the extent that the program represented an authoritative or parental entity in the eyes of the college community.

Because mental health staff are exposed, in their interpersonal relationships with professional colleagues, to a combined dosage of lofty admiration and implacable contempt, they are frequently under great social pressure to demonstrate their own, highly imperfect humanness. To be effective on an interpersonal level, however, they must constantly be vigilant in recognizing the effects of transference upon

their interpersonal relations with professional colleagues.

The Role of Frustration and Disappointment with One's Own Psychotherapy as a Resistance to Mental Health Services

Certain members of the staff of a college may regard the mental health service with distrust and trepidation due to their own unfortunate prior ex- perience with psychotherapy. Because psychotherapy is an intricate process of interaction between two or more complex personalities, even the best method of treatment does not necessarily produce satisfactory results, at least not immediately. Mental health practitioners are continually confronted with the doeful accounts of many patients who regularly report their dissatisfactions and disappointments with the therapy and the therapist. To a degree, these accounts may be distorted and exaggerated, or they may be quite natural manifestations of a painful psychological pro- cess which is intrinsically plagued by periodic dis- illusionment.

On the other hand, as most candid mental health practitioners will readily admit, psychotherapeutic failures may also result from the ineptitude or incompetence of the psychotherapist. Flaws in the psychotherapist's training or personality can interfere with or perhaps even destroy a patient's considerable potential for psychological improvement. A myopic or uncharitable psychotherapist may self-servingly attribute all cases of psychotherapeutic failure to his patients' "resistances" to personal change and growth.

During my tenure as an administrator of the Mental Health Program I have detected that some college personnel assumed an almost immediate belligerence or aversion toward the MHP. In my later dealings with them or with some of their intimates on the campus, I discovered that some of these individuals had previously suffered relatively serious personal crises and, in their view, had been treated shabbily by mental health professionals. In most instances I could not clearly perceive whether their bitter and antagonistic attitudes were the result of the gross mishandling of their personal difficulties by mental health professionals or were the consequence of their own regrettable inability to derive benefit from the services which were extended to them.

Whatever the causes for their abortive attempt to acquire beneficial psychological services to deal with their own psychological crises, some college personnel immediately identified the MHP with those other "egregious" and "unfit" psychotherapists who, in their view, so badly disserved them. This identification may become a potent factor in engendering strong resistance among certain college personnel to the mental health service.

Racial and/or Ethnic Resistances to Mental Health Services

Whenever the ethnic composition of the mental health service staff sharply contrasts with the ethnic composition of the college administration, certain tensions and disjunctions develop between the two groups. The college administration may perceive, often quite legitimately, the particular ethnic mix of the mental health service as an implied criticism of their traditional hiring practices. This ethnic mix may also be viewed as a dangerous harbinger of incremental changes in the hiring of minorities which will markedly alter the heretofore homogeneous racial composition of the college administration.

Particularly in the earliest years of the MHP, the highest positions in the college administration were occupied, almost exclusively, by White, Catholic men. Concurrently, at least one-half of the staff of the MHP was composed of minority professionals. The racial and ethnic contrast between the MHP and the college administration created an administrative disunion which was manifested in a variety of ways.

For example, as indicated earlier, the largely White college administration deemed only the White administrator of the MHP (me) capable of possessing aggressive and nonconformist qualities. The Asian administrator (Ms. Quan Holden) was immune to charges of aggressively "politicizing" the MHP's struggles for permanency, because the college administration, as a group of White dominant males, was unable to acknowledge that an Asian woman could be "scrutably" and politically assertive.

Another manifestation of the ethnic breach between the MHP and the college administration was the social distance which existed between the two groups. As mentioned earlier, the Dean of Students had almost no social intercourse with the MHP staff. His interactions with the MHP were almost entirely confined to the exchange of pragmatic instructions and information. With minority members of the MHP, the Dean was even more socially aloof, scarcely reciprocating with them more than a friendly greeting.

301

A third manifestation of the ethnic disjunction between the MHP and the college administration takes the form of simplistic and unrealistic expectations that the college administrators had of minority MHP professionals. As a Black psychotherapist in the MHP remarked, "Members of the (White) administration often believe that Black psychotherapists have an omniscient understanding of, and magical solutions to, the problems of all other Blacks. Thus, they frequently impose unrealistic expectations upon the Black psychotherapist, which frequently he cannot meet."

When a largely White college administration remains socially aloof from an ethnically integrated MHP, it affords itself relatively few opportunities to acquire those personal experiences which are necessary correctives to its racial biases. For example, the Dean requested a small and inexperienced Hispanic trainee to intervene in a conflict between a Chicano student and his physical education instructor. As mentioned earlier, the employment of the trainee in such a situation was clearly inappropriate and potentially dangerous.

I think the Dean's unreasonable request was, to an extent, the inevitable consequence of his social estrangement from the MHP. Because he had little interpersonal association with the MHP, he had never met the trainee; thus, he had no opportunity to acquire a realistic conception of her clinical skills and limitations. Consequently, he was forced to depend upon his own inferences about an unknown minority trainee, which were largely based upon stereotypical conceptions of her as a "sample specimen" of a "reified" group.

The Dean's conception was that minority clinicians can immediately understand and smoothly resolve the psychological conflicts of students who have cultural backgrounds which are similar to their own, irrespective of the complexity of the conflicts. Because the Dean had no first-hand acquaintance with minority staff of the MHP, he not only misconceived their potentialities, but was also able to immunize his misconceptions from potentially corrective interpersonal experiences, i.e., through close interpersonal association with minority staff. In a vicious circle, his misconceptions led to unrealistic expectations of the minority staff. Such expectations were, predictably, disappointed. Disappointment bred rage, which ultimately developed into another source of formidable resistance.

The Wish to be a Psychotherapist, as a Source of Re-

The profession of the college psychotherapist
is usually a fascinating, challenging and personally
rewarding one. The enthusiasm and interest with which
the campus psychotherapist performs and publicly dis-
cusses his work often provoke the envy of those of his
professional colleagues who are, to any degree, disgruntled by their organizational assignments. Thus,
the campus psychotherapist may be viewed, with good
reason, as the possessor of an enviable livelihood.

I have discerned, on innumerable occasions, the
strong wishes of professional colleagues to learn and
perform psychotherapeutic services. Because this wish
frequently remains unfulfilled, and therefore serves
as a source of personal frustration, it may become
transmuted into resentment and resistance to those who
work in the college mental health service.

For example, in the earliest years of the MHP, I
received visits from several counselors and instructors,
all of whom requested employment in the MHP. All of
these requests stemmed from dissatisfactions with current assignments and a wish to enter a new, exciting
profession. Applicants invariably expressed a wish to
occupy a professional niche in which they could "really"
help students, instead of "spinning their wheels" on

304

their present assignments. They each envisaged a mental health position as one in which they could, at last, be important to the lives of students and, at the same time, derive useful psychological insights about themselves and others.

For administrative and political reasons, I rejected the applicants' requests. I did this as tactfully and as supportively as I could, explaining that the chairpersons and deans of their respective departments would undoubtedly resent and protest our wresting their personnel from assignments for which they were originally hired. I also encouraged each applicant to explore the possibilities of diversifying and enhancing his present assignment, perhaps by discussing his chronic dissatisfactions with his departmental colleagues. I added, quite correctly I believe, that hiring personnel from other departments would ultimately have dire consequences for the MHP, which would far outweigh any benefits which could be accrued from their employment. My opinion was based upon the fact that there was no college-wide career development program which encouraged lateral movement between departments.

I learned, soon after several of these interviews, that the applicants were furious with me. I was told by their departmental peers that I had ex-

305

hibited a disrespect for their competency and know-how. They considered my rejections to be crass aspersions upon their professional capabilities. In short, they were humiliated and offended by my adverse response to their aspirations for a more fulfilling professional career. It is no coincidence, I believe, that, to the best of my knowledge, none of the applicants has referred any students to the MHP for psychotherapy since the time when they were denied entry into the program. Their aspirations to become psychotherapists having been denied, were transformed into resistances to mental health services.

VII

SURVIVAL SKILLS FOR THE MENTAL HEALTH
PROGRAM ADMINISTRATOR

Pursuant to the purpose of this study, as stated in Chapter I, I have attempted to identify and interpret the manifold forces within an academic institution which impacted upon the mental health program in its developmental stages. I have attempted to demonstrate the axiom that in order to dynamically understand an organization, one must understand those personalities which have gained leadership and dominance over that organization. In this study I have described the recurrent and intense interactions between a college administration, which I have characterized as authoritarian, and a mental health program, which I have described as humanistic. I have found it most helpful and appropriate to use two particular theoretical frameworks in order to describe and explain the administrative leadership of the college: (1) the psychoanalytic model which explains the authoritarian personality's idiosyncratic use of psychological defense mechanisms, and

307

(2) Victor Thompson's (1971) hypothesis that all modern organizations develop certain "bureaupathic" (authoritarian) tendencies as they become more specialized and complex.

I consider the choice of using these two theoretical frameworks to analyze my data to be a sound and appropriate one. They have enabled me to acquire a dynamic perspective of the authoritarian personality in his professional role in the academic institution. They have also enabled me to understand the complex nature of the impact of the authoritarian personality upon the growth and development of the mental health program and upon me, both professionally and personally. These theoretical frameworks help to explain, I believe, how different people react quite differently to authoritarian leadership. For example, if the staff of the mental health program had conformed to the expectations of the college administration, the mental health program would not have survived and this paper would not have been written.

The process of describing and explaining in this paper the organizing and sustaining of the Mental Health Program has been a personally exacting one for me. Because I have attached great emotional importance to the events described in this study, it has been imperative for me to exercise rigorous self-discipline and self-detachment in order to write a work of genuine scholarship, rather than a rancorous diatribe. At times the recollection and recording of painful events, such as my threat of legal action against the SHS Coordinator, had an uplifting, almost cathartic effect upon me. In recording such incidents, I frequently felt unrealistically indestructible and triumphant. On the other hand, in recalling the overpowering humiliations which Ms. Quan Holden and I had suffered at the hands of the college administration, I often felt a murderous rage which temporarily impaired my powers of recall, reasoning and articulation.

I was vastly assisted during moments of confusion and anger by my informants, who were uniformly cooperative and generous with their time and information. Through their generous assistance they were able to supplement and objectify my own recollections of the events described in this study. More importantly, however, their lively interest in the outcome of the study and their enthusiastically expressed wishes to read the final document guided me positively toward the goal of writing as detailed, candid and objective a study as I was capable of achieving. I am profoundly grateful to my informants for the material and emotion-

al assistance which they extended to me in this endeav-
or.

A critic of this study might assert that it is
too one-sided, or too monodramatic; that it depicts,
almost propagandistically, the college administration
as inordinately   monolithic and malevolent. Such a
critic might ask, "Wasn't there anything redeeming
about the college administration which deserved mention in this study? I will attempt to answer that
question by referring to the following considerations.

First, one purpose of my study was to describe
and analyze those characteristics which distinguish the
authoritarian personality from the humanistic personality. The college administration was not uniformly
authoritarian in its behaviors and attitudes toward
the MHP. For example, recall the Chancellor-Superintendent's encouragement to procure permanent MHP positions from other academic departments. This gesture
was perceived by Ms. Quan Holden and me as genuinely
humanistic. By the same token, the staff of the MHP
were not consistently humanistic in behavior and attitude, either toward one another or toward the college administration. When I was feeling particularly
oppressed or persecuted by the college administration,
my own behavior could become abrasive and authoritar-

310

ian. Recall, for example, my autocratic appointment of Ms. Quan Holden to an administrative position in the MHP.

Nevertheless, one intent in this study is to adumbrate the overall distinguishing features of the authoritarian personality. What distinguishes the authoritarian personality from the humanistic personality is his unremitting and involuntary proclivity to manifest behavior and attitudes which are sexist, ethnocentric and punitive. The fact that he is also capable of periodic manifestations of tenderness, sincerity and goodwill (humanism) attests to his basic humanness, but does not negate his basic personality structure. The basic structure of the authoritarian personality, as I have here attempted to describe and analyze it, is rigid, power-oriented and potentially exploitative of others, i.e., qualitatively different from the humanistic personality. This is obviously an unflattering characterization; however, the authoritarian personality, at least to the humanist, is an objectionable and, at times, even socially dangerous individual.

A second factor which affects the "one-sided" characterization of the college administration in this study is the intentionally limited scope of the study itself. The study does not encompass the college administration's relationships to other college programs, nor do I, for example, attempt to understand the nature of the college administration's personal relationships. Presumably, many of their professional colleagues and some of their own family members regarded the college administrators who were discussed in this study as humane, considerate and nurturing individuals.

Nevertheless, the staff of the MHP were in a relatively unique and "advantageous" position to experience and witness the "worst" aspects of the college administration's authoritarianism. The MHP's vantage point was provided by the fact that it, perhaps more than any other program in the entire history of City College, confronted and combatted the *power* of the college administration. By doing so, it naturally would incite and incur the full fury of a power-oriented college administration. This kind of experience, in my view, gave the staff of the MHP a singular opportunity to acquire a penetrating, if seemingly "one-sided," understanding of the authoritarianism of the college administration.

The position of the MHP relative to the college administration might be likened to that of the relatively defenseless child in a tyrannical home. Such a child might be treated well, providing that he uncomplainingly conforms to the wishes and demands of his authoritarian parents. Perhaps his siblings opt for such a *modus vivendi*, in exchange for security, affection, material assistance; that is, love. However, if the child chooses to deviate from the authoritarian constraints of his parents, he will incur criticism, contempt, and perhaps even abandonment; that is, loss of love. If he has sufficient ego strength, he may be willing to face the prospect of the loss of parental love for the sake of maintaining his personal integrity and independence.

I believe the above-mentioned analogy aptly illustrates the peculiar position of the MHP *vis-a-vis* the college administration. Unquestionably, certain other departments of City College did not perceive the college administration as malevolent or punitive. For example, the Counseling Department, in my estimation, had, for the most part, a highly favorable attitude toward the Chancellor-Superintendent and his administrative supporters. I here remind the reader of the aforementioned comments of a dean who stated that various ethnically prejudiced counselors had been respected and protected by the college administration for many years. Such a generous *quid pro quo* would hardly cause those

counselors to view the college administration as dis-
obliging or punitive.

The MHP, on the other hand, unlike most other
college departments, had directly and forcefully challenged the authority and power of the college administration to undertake unilateral decisions regarding the
future status of its staff. This challenge penetrated
to the core of the authoritarian personality's foremost
concern: the threat of the loss of personal power. As
a result, the MHP in particular (as the independent and
disfavored "child") was disproportionately exposed to
the "worst" characteristics of the authoritarian personality: sexism, racism, and punitive aggression. Since
it was this kind of behavior which was most commonly
and observably manifested toward the MHP, the "one-
sided" nature of this study is, I believe, an accurate
and valid assessment of an authoritarian college administration undergoing a formidable challenge to its authority and power.

The findings in this study are generally consistent with the conclusions regarding the authoritarian
personality which have been reported by Adorno, *et al.*
(1950). These findings depict the authoritarian personality as an individual who is characterized by a particular syndrome, or group of idiosyncratic attributes.

314

These attributes are: punitive aggressiveness, cynicism, inordinate concern with personal strength, distrust of tender feelings, and a tendency to view the world in categorical, conventional and moralistic terms. In addition, the authoritarian personality is inclined to be ethnocentric, i.e., he regards members of outgroups as alien, deviant, or weak. He also tends to view and treat women with contempt; contempt particularly for their own creativity and individuality. The interpersonal relationships of the authoritarian personality tend to be shallow and based less on personal experience and feelings than on conventions and stereotypes. The authoritarian personality tends to handle his impulses through extensive use of denial, repression, displacement and counter-cathexes, rather than by means of sublimation.

Obviously, the above-mentioned attributes do not necessarily hang together in all authoritarian individuals, since the "authoritarian personality" is a theoretical character type. Nevertheless, these attributes are discovered with sufficient frequency and intensity in certain power-oriented individuals to warrant the characterization of such persons as "authoritarian" personalities.

Authoritarian personalities enter and shape all

315

kinds of social organizations. However, the intrinsic
nature of the contemporary social organization also
accounts, to a considerable extent, for the authoritarian behavior which is evident in all social systems.
Thompson (1971) suggests that certain "bureaupathic"
(authoritarian) tendencies emerge in all bureaucratic
organizations as they become specialized. Among these
tendencies are excessive aloofness, resistance to
change, ritualistic attachment to routines and procedures and a petty insistence upon the rights of authority and status.

Tannenbaum (1966) asserts that the formal organization is designed to minimize or eliminate disruptions caused by individual idiosyncracy. He suggests
that, from the point of view of the formal organization,
it makes no difference who performs a given role, provided that one's behavior is appropriate and conforming.

Bennis (1969) states that the bureaucratic mechanism is poorly equipped to cope with the humanistic
ethos of twentieth century conditions. As a result,
the contemporary social organization attempts to integrate individual needs and management goals by regarding the individual as a passive instrument (authoritarianism), rather than as a complex being with rising expectations (humanism). In coping with the problem of

316

the distribution of power, the bureaucratic organization tends to implicitly use coercive authority rather than education and a shared decision-making process. The bureaucratic solution to the problem of resolving conflicts is the exploitation of "loyalty" rather than reliance on competence and professionalism. More succinctly, Pfiffner and Sherwood (1960), refer to the large-scale social organization as potentially "a standardizing enemy of human dignity."

Erving Goffman (1961), in referring to "total institutions" such as the mental hospital, avers that the occupational roles of those who administer such organizations crush the psychiatric patient "by the weight of a service ideal that eases life for the rest of us."

In alluding to a similar phenomenon in a child-care agency in which I formerly worked, Amada (1972) identified some of the following organizational problems: (1) a general tendency of administrators to carry out decisions in a unilateral and coercive manner, (2) an uncooperative attitude on the part of administrators toward the recommendations of referring agencies for therapeutic planning and rehabilitation, and (3) institutional racism as manifested in a policy of refusing admission of minority children to the child-care

317

program,

Sigmund Freud (1921) argues that all social units, including large, complex organizations, symbolize the family matrix to their members. According to Freud, as members join the social organization, they begin a process of psychological regression. In a childlike manner, they relegate to the leader of the organization the functions of a parent, and thus the whole process of emotional maturation is reversed. Under the spell of a strong leader, the member of a social organization becomes a dependent child.

If we accept Freud's postulate, authoritarianism in social organizations results, in part, from the regressive insecurities of subordinates who are ready to relinquish their social freedoms for the security promised by strong leaders. In other words, authoritarian leaders hold and exercise unilateral power, to a degree, through the deference of their organizational subordinates.

Morowitz (1977) views (I believe with his tongue partially in his cheek) social organizations as ecological systems in which there are "primary producers" (the lower organisms) who occupy the bottom of the organizational chart. Top management or the "carnivores" can gain their sustenance and professional success by

318

"preying" upon lower carnivores (middle management), who, in turn, are predators of the primary producers. Al- though Morowitz states that the ecological model he has formulated is morally neutral, he does imply that human beings develop personal characteristics which are appropriate to their organizational "niches." Thus, the primary producers behave and think like a down- trodden species and the administrative leaders like pred- ators.

Classical organizational theory, as explained by Etzioni (1964), has made the division of labor its central tenet. The division of labor, within the organ- izational structure, must be balanced by a unity of con- trol. Classical theorists view the pyramidal organiza- tional sturcture with one center of authority as a ra- tional and efficient mechanism with which to optimize productivity and minimize costs.

Some Conclusions Regarding Authoritarianism in the College

There are several important factors which account for the authoritarianism of academic institutions in particular. First, academic institutions are often viewed as commodities which are subject to the princi- pals of supply and demand. In other words, the college is sometimes perceived as a business. Nevertheless, as Reinhert (1972) states, "One of the factors that distinguishes a university (or college) from a manufacturing business is that increased production does not result in the mass production economies a manufacturer would achieve" (p. 49). Yet all academic institutions must contend with the rising costs of instruction, construction, and maintenance. Although there is no necessary connection between educational success and financial success, obviously a degree of the latter is imperative for sustaining the institution. Because innovation is likely to drive per capita costs up, administrators of colleges which are in financial straits must discourage or oppose institutional change. Such administrators may become preoccupied with questions of cost and efficiency, while ignoring vital concerns such as the quality of educational programs and the learning atmosphere of the institution.

In my estimation, the conflict between the MHP and the City College administration was based, in part, upon a difference in outlook regarding the matter of cost effectiveness. Most mental health programs are intrinsically expensive and their cost effectiveness cannot be measured accurately. At best, one could evaluate the cost effectiveness of a men-

320

tal health program only through meticulous longitudinal studies which followed and evaluated the clients of such programs for many years. Even then, such studies could not determine the cost effectiveness of such programs with an exactitude sufficient to allay the concerns of fiscally troubled college administrators.

A second factor which propels college administrations toward authoritarianism is the doctrine of *in loco parentis*. In recent years there has been a steady and strong progression toward the augmentation of the civil rights of students. Historically, however, colleges have assumed and wielded parental prerogatives in order to monitor and govern freedom of speech, sexual conduct, dresswear, drug use and abuse, and the rights to privacy of students. As Laudicina and Tramutola (1974) suggest, "In actual fact, the doctrine of *in loco parentis* was a convenient fiction utilized to buttress the sometimes questionable authority of college officialdom" (p. 7).

Today there are two factors in particular which militate against the principle of *in loco parentis*: (1) the demands of students to participate in and assume a degree of control over the decisions which affect their academic careers, and (2) the rules of the community within which the college resides have taken priority over the rules of the college itself. "No longer, for example, can college administrators develop effective rules separate from those that have been formulated by civic officials" (Laudicina & Tramutola, 1974, p. 7). Many regulations such as the right to carry firearms are now subject to judicial consideration.

Nevertheless, I believe it would be fatuous to ignore the fact that college administrators do and must retain some of the vestiges of parental power over students. In many respects the college is a fiduciary *vis-a-vis* the student. The fiduciary concept assumes that the college is a repository of administrative authority entrusted by its charter to formulate rules and manage resources for the benefit of students. The rules and regulations which govern student rights may be found in institutional bulletins and catalogues. Admission procedures, rules regarding personal behavior, curriculum prerogatives and graduation requirements are all examples of those areas in which the college administrator exercises a form of parental authority.

Although the assumption and use of parental authority does not necessarily lead to authoritarianism, such power places a great onus upon its possessor. For example, can an administrator who possesses parental power over students, and who is beholden to administrative superiors for carrying out that power, also be an advocate for students? Such a prospect is entirely conceivable. I have observed many City College administrators advocate the rights of students, even when the students' cause was a generally unpopular one. However, I have also observed that such administrators must frequently anguish over such advocacy of students, since their "official" task is to enforce "parental" rules which sometimes conflict with the rights of students. Unless the administrator has sufficient ego strength and personal integrity, he may opt to carry out his official responsibilities with relative disregard for the rights of students, whom he perhaps perceives as (his) children, and thereby fall prone to authoritarian behavior. When he does, he will inevitably clash with programs such as the MHP which regard and treat students as adults with affirmable rights to self-determination.

Another factor which generates and reinforces authoritarianism in college administrations are the inequities of the hierarchical system which is inherent in the college. College administrators commonly are long-time and loyal stalwarts, many of whom were appointed to their administrative posts precisely as rewards for their loyalty and longevity. Perhaps, too, they were selected because they had already demonstrated a toughness or authoritarianism in their former professional capacity which appeared especially to qualify them for assuming extensive administrative authority. Because his appointment to an administrative position was not, strictly speaking, meritorious, an administrator may continue to rely upon those personal qualities for which he was originally rewarded: loyalty and conformity.

Further inducements to authoritarianism within the hierarchical system of the college are inequities in power, vocational perquisites, prestige and financial remuneration. Generally, as one moves up the organizational hierarchy of the college, administrative power increases (i.e., in the form of the control of departmental budgets), vocational emoluments improve (such as the acquisition of superior office facilities), prestige grows (as reflected by the greater recognition one receives from colleagues, friends and family), and income rises (since college salaries are usually commensurate with one's years of professional experience and rise dramatically when one enters the administrative ranks).

As college administrators derive the benefits of longevity and loyalty, they may perceive themselves as a privileged hegemonic class and their organizational subordinates as a disenfranchised underclass. Such a social perspective breeds and reflects authoritarianism. In this context, the contention between the City College administration and the MHP (a relatively powerless organizational entity) might validly be viewed as a form of (social) class conflict.

One final point, which I have already briefly touched upon, is the process by which college administrators are selected to their positions. This process can be a principal source of institutional authoritarianism, for two reasons. First, if we can safely assume that authoritarian individuals quest for power more diligently and ambitiously than humanistic individuals, it is likely that the authoritarian personality will more readily gravitate toward administrative assignments, since the primary locus of power in the college lies within the administrative ranks.

Second, if the administrative positions of the college especially attract and hold authoritarian individuals, these authoritarian personalities, once they become entrenched in their administrative positions, will tend to prefer other authoritarian character types who share their orientation to power. Thus, they will selectively recruit individuals much like themselves to additional administrative posts and thereby augment and solidify the authoritarianism of the college.

Mental health program administrators who aspire to provide effective services to college students will frequently encounter strong resistances to their professional efforts from authoritarian college administrations. In order to adequately meet the psychological needs of students, it may be necessary to oppose the demands and expectations of such college administrations. Therefore, it is incumbent upon the administrators of mental health programs to develop personal and professional skills and strategies with which to cope effectively with authoritarian administrations.

Skills of the College Mental Health Service Administrator

An infinite number of professional and personal skills and strengths are required of those who seek to organize and sustain college mental health services. I will refer to those capabilities which I think were of particular relevance to Ms. Quan Holden and me.

Psychodynamic Understanding

In many respects, the role of the campus psychotherapist is analogous to, and compatible with, the
role of the mental health program administrator. In
order to overcome the many organizational resistances
to the mental health service, the program administrator must acquire an understanding of the unconscious
motivations of his professional colleagues which will
necessarily color their manifest attitudes toward him
and his program.

Ms. Quan Holden and I spent many worthwhile
hours discussing and defining the latent motivations
and intentions of our organizational adversaries. Our
ability to decipher motivational factors was fruitful
in several respects:

(1) It provided rational insights into organizational behavior which would otherwise seem inexplic-
able or even bizarre. This ability, therefore, helped
to reduce our sense of impotent bewilderment which we
periodically experienced as a result of perplexing
organizational resistances to our programmatic efforts.

(2) Our psychological insights provided Ms. Quan
Holden and me with a certain predictive prowess. For
example, our psychological assessment of the SHS Coordinator led us to believe that she lacked an ap-

327

propriate degree of guilt in her administration of harsh treatment toward the MHP. Her insatiable quest for power and its accoutrements made our appeals to her sense of fair play, justice, or morality quite futile.

Ms. Quan Holden and I gradually acquired a realization that the SHS Coordinator would behave responsibly toward the MHP only when confronted with the threat, or actual use, of our own personal and professional power. Consequently, when the SHS Coordinator and I discussed her "reservations" about my prospective college employment, I was able quickly to apprehend the futility of altering her antagonistic position with rejoinders about my professional qualifications. Although my threat to gain my legal rights through litigation was neither idle nor unemotional, it was, to a large extent, a premeditated action. I anticipated that an appeal to a higher authority (the power of the courts) would be the strongest antidote to her ambitions to propitiate the college administration by ousting me.

I think the SHS Coordinator's irresolute behavior during the proceedings of the Mental Health Hiring Committee, during which she allowed my name to be entered as a job finalist, indicated that our

psychological insights regarding her unconscious motivations and susceptibilities, were largely correct.

(3) The conceptual grasping of motivational
factors assisted Ms. Quan Holden and me in another
important respect. The various forms of organizational
opposition to the MHP were often painfully disheartening to us. The repeated and malevolent condemnations
of our behavior often intimidated us, and dampened our
optimism, at least temporarily. However, by quickly
and jointly undertaking a psychodynamic investigation
of the motives of our organizational antagonists, Ms.
Quan Holden and I were able to rebound from our dol-
drums. Through such investigations we were able to
perceive our adversaries more realistically and, by
doing so, we were also able to overcome our feelings
that we were genuine pariahs on the campus. Frequently, our self-esteem and morale rested upon securing an
accurate conceptual assessment of the psychological
motives of our opponents.

An Inalienable Administrative Partnership

Although I held somewhat more official administrative authority in the MHP than Ms. Quan Holden, we
functioned, on a day-to-day basis, as administrative
equals. All crucial administrative decisions were made

jointly. There were many attempts to "divide and con-
quer" us, all of which bore no fruit. For example, the
SHS Coordinator attempted to enlist Ms. Quan Holden's
cooperation in keeping her "reservations" about me
confidential. During the months immediately preceding
the adoption of the MHP, the Dean of Students would
rather flamboyantly remark that perhaps only one of us
would be hired and the other terminated.

These attempts to drive an unwholesome wedge
between Ms. Quan Holden and me were counteracted by
our ongoing dialogue, which specifically addressed
the matter of our opponents' divisive tactics. Our
conferences invariably ended with renewed pledges to
support one another, regardless of the personal or professional consequences. Although our opinions and
perspectives were, at times, discrepant, Ms. Quan Holden and I maintained an unflinching respect for each
other's points of view. By maintaining an inalienable
administrative partnership, we strengthened our individual convictions and determination to surmount all
organizational obstacles to our programmatic objectives.

The Recognition and Acknowledgement of Countertrans-
ference Feelings

As indicated earlier, the organizational resistances to the college mental health service, to a great extent, represented transference attitudes which the program animated by its authoritative presence on the campus. Consequently, the staff of the MHP were exposed, on an interpersonal level, to a wide range of intense emotions. As a result, the MHP staff were prone, as they might be during the course of a psychotherapeutic session, to harboring equally intense countertransference feelings for their professional colleagues. In other words, the organizational resistances to their efforts would frequently cause the MHP staff to feel as if they were engaging in earlier rivalries or conflicts with their own siblings or parents.

Such feelings were natural and inevitable; however, if they were not adequately understood or appreciated, countertransference attitudes could have adverse affects upon one's professional performance. For example, in dealing with our administrative superordinates, Ms. Quan Holden and I frequently had irrational feelings of powerlessness and vindictiveness, such as we often felt as children. In those moments, we recognized that we were attributing inordinate power and control to our administrative superiors and, conversely, too little to ourselves. Together and separately, we often traced the sources of our anxieties and conflicts to earlier adverse experiences of our respective childhoods. Frequently, this careful introspection uncovered considerable personal material which proved valuable in overcoming our fears.

For example, as the youngest of four sons, I grew up with frequent feelings of insecurity about my intelligence and importance. When I felt particularly barraged by criticisms or allegations from the college administration, my psychological associations with those childhood experiences caused me to doubt my competency and worth. By discovering and addressing the original sources of my "neurotic" fears, I could regain a realistic perspective of my personal strengths and resources.

I think the administrator of the college mental health service must attend to his countertransference feelings as much during the course of his administrative activities as he does during the course of his psychotherapeutic work, if he is to be a successful administrator.

Respect for a Multiethnic and Multidisciplinary Mental Health Staff

The administrator of a multiethnic and multidisciplinary staff is faced with many formidable challenges to his personal stability and integrity. Each professional discipline and each ethnic group will earnestly and justifiably vie to extol its accomplishments and worth to the program. Each, as it should, will take intense pride in its professional or cultural uniqueness, and consequently, will often seek to augment its status and influence in the program.

To be effective at the administrative helm of an ethnically and professionally heterogeneous staff, one must respect the singular contributions of the respective disciplinary and ethnic groups which are represented in the program. This respect may be demonstrated in tangible terms such as through the affirmative hiring of minority professionals. Perhaps more importantly, however, the program administrator may demonstrate his respect by understanding and acknowledging that, no matter how professionally or personally dedicated he is to the principle of racial equality, he will not be immediately accepted as an ally by all members of an ethnically diverse staff. On the contrary, the White mental health service administrator, such as myself, will sometimes be perceived as the embodiment of the many individual and institutional oppressors of minority peoples which exist throughout American society.

Consequently, the White administrator of an ethnically integrated mental health service must examine his own feelings, attitudes and behaviors for ethnic biases. He must be psychologically resilient and prepared for the wariness of others towards both his authoritative role and his whiteness. When he is unfairly charged with ethnic insensitivity or even racism, there is little point in referring to the painful discrimination he may have suffered throughout his lifetime. He must be patient and not expect to quickly cement friendships with those who suspect his motives and ideals. If he is not too eager to be universally liked and appreciated, he will not feel the rebuffs he will inevitably receive too keenly. If he is truly not a culpable administrator in his interactions with ethnic staff members, he need not admit to culpability. However, he must recognize and respect the need of many minority people, impatient with years of fruitless waiting for equal opportunity and a voice in the decisions which affect their daily lives, to doubt his sincerity and offers of friendship.

I think it appropriate to mention at this point that my feelings and thoughts on this issue have changed considerably over the years. When I first entered the MHP, I believed that my humanistic and libertarian ideals and intentions were as obvious to others as they were to me. I believed that, through hard work and courageous commitment, I would receive an unanimous appreciation for my professional efforts. Even more naively, I expected heartfelt gratitude and admiration from the various beneficiaries of my leadership of the MHP. These hopes and wishes were, in the final analysis, more egocentric than altruistic. For me, at this time, the mere realization that the unity and success of the professionally and ethnically diverse MHP have been, to some extent, the outgrowth of my own administrative leadership, is ample reward for the many maddening and disheartening setbacks I had to endure as the program director.

REFERENCES

Adorno, T.W., *et al.* *The authoritarian personality.*
New York: John Wiley & Sons, 1966.

Amada, G. Social work in a college mental health program. *Social Casework,*1972, *53*(9).

Amada, G. Crisis-oriented psychotherapy. *Journal
of Contemporary Psychotherapy,* 1977, *9*(1).

Anspacher, C. State blasts San Francisco over mental
health programs. *San Francisco Chronicle,* April
29, 1975.

Bennis, W. Changing organizations. In Bennis, *et al.*
(Eds.), *The planning of change.* New York: Holt,
Rinehart & Winston, 1969.

Binger, A.L. Emotional disturbances among women. In
Blain, G. Jr., & McArthur, C. C. (Eds.), *Emotional
problems of the student.* New York: Appleton-
Century-Crofts, 1961.

Brook, G. L. *Varieties of English.* New York: Mac-
millan, 1973.

Carey, J. Correspondence to a community agency, March
20, 1969.

Carey, J. Correspondence to the City College President.

Conlon, L. Letter to community agency, May, 1969

Dillard, J.L. *Black English.* New York: Random House,
1972

Downs, A. *Inside bureaucracy.* Boston: Little, Brown
& Co., 1967.

Drews, E. M. Self-actualization: A new focus for ed-
ucation. In Waetzen, W. B., & Leeper, R. R.
(Eds.), *Learning and mental health in the school.*
Washington, D.C.: Association for Supervision and
Curriculum Development, 1966.

336

Etzioni, A. *Modern organizations*. Englewood Cliffs, N.J.: Prentice-Hall, 1964.

Evans, N., & Neagley, R. L. *Planning and developing innovative community colleges*. Englewood Cliffs, N.J.: Prentice-Hall, 1973.

Farnsworth, D. L. *Mental health in college and university*. Cambridge, Mass.: Harvard University Press, 1957.

Farnsworth, D. L. *College health administration*. New York: Appleton-Century-Crofts, 1964.

Fenichel, O. *The psychoanalytic theory of neurosis*. New York: W.W. Norton & Co., 1945.

Friedman, M. *The college experience*. San Francisco: Jossey-Bass, 1967.

Freud, A. *The ego and the mechanisms of defense*. Vol. II. New York: International Universities Press, 1936.

Freud, S. *Group Psychology and the analysis of the ego*. London: Hogarth Press, 1921.

Fujitomi, I., & Wong, D. The new Asian-American woman. In Sue, S., & Wagner, N. (Eds.), *Asian-Americans, psychological perspectives*. Palo Alto, CA.: Science and Behavior Books, 1973.

Gerth, H. H., & Mills, C.W. (Eds.). *From Max Weber: Essays in sociology*. New York: Oxford University Press, 1970.

Glasscote, R., *et al*. *Mental health on the campus*. Washington, D.C.: Joint Information Service of American Psychiatric Association and the National Association for Mental Health, 1973.

Goffman, E. *Asylums*. Garden City, N.Y.: Doubleday & Co., 1961.

Gove, P. B. (Ed.). *Webster's third new international dictionary*. Springfield, Mass.: G & C Merrian Co., 1970.

337

Hayakawa, S. I. *Language in thought and action.* New York: Harcourt, Brace & World, 1964.

Hills, R. J. *Toward a science of organization.* Eugene, Ore.: University of Oregon, 1968.

Holden, M. Personal communication to the author, 1977.

Laudicina, R., & Tramutola, J. L. *A legal perspective for student personnel administrators.* Springfield, Ill.: Charles C. Thomas, 1974.

Leavitt, A., Carey, J., & Swartz, J. Developing a mental health program at an urban community college. *Journal of the American College Health Association,* 1971, *19,* 200.

Leavitt, A. Conversation with the author, June, 1977.

Leavitt, A., & Curry, A. Training minority mental health professionals. *Hospital and Community Psychiatry,* 1973, *24,* 8.

Lewin, K. *Brief encounters.* St. Louis: Warren H. Green, Inc., 1970.

Likert, R. Motivational approach to organization. In Haire, M. (Ed.), *Modern organization theory.* New York: John Wiley & Sons, 1959.

Moore, W., Jr. *Blind man on a freeway.* San Francisco, CA.: Jossey -Bass, 1971.

Morowitz, H. H. *Ego niches.* Woodbridge, Conn.: Ox Bow Press, 1977.

Orwell, G. Politics and the English language. In Thompson, D., & Hicks, J. (Eds.), *Thought and Experience in prose.* New York: Oxford University Press, 1956.

Perlman, D. A joint project for total mental health care. *San Francisco Chronicle,* April 16, 1968.

Perlman, D. A lag in services for mental health. *San Francisco Chronicle,* February 24, 1975.

Pfiffner, J., & Sherwood, F. *Administrative organization.* Englewood Cliffs, N.J.: Prentice-Hall, 1960.

Reinert, P. C. *To turn the tide.* Englewood Cliffs, N.J.: Prentice-Hall, 1972.

Ryker, M. Group work with students in a university mental health service. *Journal of the American College Health Association,* 1970, *18,* 296.

Shein, E. H. The mechanism of change. In Bennis, *et al.* (Eds.), *The planning of change.* New York: Holt, Rinehart & Winston, 1969.

Swartz, J. (Ed.) *All health to the people: Second year.* San Francisco: City College of San Francisco, 1972.

Schwartz, M. Students run a creative city college health service. *San Francisco Chronicle,* January 21, 1972.

Szasz, T. The psychiatrist as double agent. In Strauss, L. (Ed.), *Where medicine fails.* New Brunswick, N.J.: Transaction Books, 1973.

Tannenbaum, A.S. *Social psychology of the work organization.* Belmont, CA.: Wadsworth Publishing Co., 1966.

Thompson, V. Bureaucracy and bureaupathology. In Hinton, B. L., & Reitz, H. J. (Eds.), *Groups and organizations.* Belmont, CA.: Wadsworth Publishing Co., 1971.

Watsen, G. Resistance to change. In Bennis, *et al.* (Eds.), *The planning of change.* New York: Holt, Rinehart & Winston, 1969.

Wong, J. S. *Fifth Chinese daughter.* New York: Harper & Row, 1945.

APPENDIX

Correspondence

Amada, G. To County Supervisor, Feb. 14, 1974.

Amada, G. To Medical Director, California Medical
Clinic for Psychotherapy, May 15, 1973.

Amada, G. To Trustee, Bothin Helping Fund, Jan. 25,
1974.

Clinical Coordinator and Author. To City College
Faculty, June 7, 1974.

Copely Newspapers, Spring, 1974.

Executive Director, Bothin Helping Fund, Feb. 20,
1974.

Executive Director, WCMHS, June 21, 1974.

Executive Director, Zellerbach Family Fund, Dec. 26,
1973.

Executive Director, Zellerbach Family Fund. To Governor F., Spring, 1974.

Louis R. Lurie Foundation, Spring, 1974.

Medical Director, California Medical Clinic for Psychotherapy, May 21, 1973.

President, Peter Haas Fund, Jan. 3, 1974.

Program Chief, San Francisco Community Mental Health
Services. To Acting Dean of Business Affairs,
SFCC, Spring, 1975.

Public Health Nurse, SFCC. To community agency,
March 20, 1969.

S.F. County Supervisor, April 25, 1974.

Student Council. To President, SFCC, Spring, 1975.

340

Memoranda

Amada, G. To President, SFCC, May 10, 1974.

Chairperson, Counseling Department, SFCC. To President, SFCC, April 3, 1974.

President, SFCC, June 4, 1974.

Public Health Nurse. To President, SFCC, 1968.

Personal Interviews

Administrative Director, SFCC Mental Health Program, June, 1977.

Chairperson, Personnel Committee, Faculty Senate, SFCC, August, 1977.

Chairperson, Program Committee, Suicide Prevention, August, 1977.

Clinical Assistant to Program Chief, SFCMHS, August, 1977.

Clinical Coordinator, June, 1977.

Co-Director, Mt. Zion Hospital Crisis Clinic, August, 1977.

Dean of Business Affairs, CCSF, Spring, 1975.

Director, Adult Psychiatry, Children's Hospital, August, 1977.

Enabler, SFCC, August, 1977.

Executive Director, WSCMHS, June, 1977.

Governor G., City College Board of Governors, Spring, 1974.

Managing Director, Progress Foundation, July, 1977.

Medical Director, Progress Foundation, July, 1977.

President, SFCC, August 1977.

Schwartz, M., Spring, 1975.

Staff Psychotherapist, MHP, September, 1977.

THE AUTHOR

Gerald Amada is Co-Director of the Mental Health Program, City College of San Francisco. He is also in private practice as a clinical psychologist in San Francisco. He received the M.S.W. degree at Rutgers University and Ph.D. at the Wright Institute, Berkeley, California.